Customer Satisfaction:

Tools, Techniques, and Formulas for Success

Customer Satisfaction:

Tools, Techniques, and Formulas for Success

Craig Cochran

Paton Press
Chico, California

Most Paton Press books are available at quantity discounts when purchased in bulk. For more information, contact:

Paton Press
P.O. Box 44
Chico, CA 95927-0044
Telephone: (530) 342-5480
Fax: (530) 342-5471
E-mail: *books@patonpress.com*
Web: *www.patonpress.com*

06 05 04 03 02   5 4 3 2 1

ISBN 0-9713231-4-3

Staff
Publisher.................................... Scott M. Paton
Senior Editor .... Taran March
Assistant Editor .... Heidi M. Paton
Book Cover Design .... Caylen Balmain

*Dedicated to Muriel, Brynn, and Cullen,
my most valuable customers*

The single most important thing
to remember about any enterprise
is that there are no results inside its walls.
The result of a business is
a satisfied customer.

—Peter Drucker

Contents

Acknowledgments

I would like to offer my special thanks to the following people and organizations for their assistance in the development of this book: Muriel, Brynn, and Cullen Cochran; P.C. and Linda Cochran; Lee Crayfish Coursey; Michael Stamp, SI Corp. (Chickamauga, Georgia); Thelma O'Dell; Debbie Ellis; Dr. Brett Saks, Kim Saks, Dynamic Chiropractic & Acupuncture Clinics, PC (Chandler, Arizona); John and Rocio Lancaster; Susan VanHemert, Consolidated Engineering Co. (Kennesaw, Georgia); Paolo Chiappina, Deann Desai, Dennis Kelly, Holly Lawe, Tim Israel, and the entire staff of the Economic Development Institute—Georgia Institute of Technology (Atlanta, Georgia); John Thomas; Matthew Staton; Tom Lull, Diamond Manufacturing Co. (Wyoming, Pennsylvania); Manual Palou, Lisa Kahn, Leslie Crawford, Caroline Smith, The Federal Deposit Insurance Corp. (Washington, D.C.); David Garner, Yamaha Motor Manufacturing Corp. (Newnan, Georgia); Scott Paton, Robert Green, Caylen Balmain, and the entire staff of *Quality Digest* magazine and Paton Press. Thanks also to Nick Grillo, Lee Nash, Formex Manufacturing Inc. (Lawrenceville, Georgia); J. Scott Jones, Atlanta Belting Co. (Atlanta, Georgia); Mike Diermeier, American Colloid Company (Letohatchee, Alabama); Gail Reeves, Paul Springer, NEETRAC—Georgia Institute of Technology; Donna K. Tierney, Naval Facilities Institute (San Diego, California); Steve Swinford, Cooper Lighting (Americus, Georgia); Chet Quilliams, Scientific-Atlanta (Atlanta, Georgia); Bob McAlister, Nick Ghali, T&D Remarketed Services (Alpharetta, Georgia); Cindy Stringer; Cindy Myers, Innovative Plastics Inc. (Huntsville, Alabama); Sandy Purcell, Metso Automation USA Inc. (Norcross, Georgia). Bill Williams, Best Manufacturing Co. (Menlo, Georgia), Bruce Woods, Cyndrus Inc. (New Orleans, Louisiana); NOLA (New Orleans, Louisiana); Ismael Villarreal, Morse Automotive (Cartersville, Georgia); Pam Moser, Lyle Industries (Dalton, Georgia); Andy Anderson, Apple Computer (Sacramento, California); and Lauren Thompson, Innovative Electronic Solutions (Alpharetta, Georgia).

Chapter 1

What Is Customer Satisfaction?

In This Chapter
- Defining the customer's perceptions
- Three basic truths about customer satisfaction
- The five basic tools of data gathering
- Steps for properly leveraging customer perceptions

There are as many answers for the question that heads this chapter as there are customers. Customer satisfaction can mean virtually anything. It can involve such variables as price, lead time, conformance, responsiveness, reliability, professionalism, and convenience—and it's sometimes a complicated mix of all of these and more. Industry by industry, and even across product lines, the importance of each variable can differ drastically.

The variables listed above are what people most often think of as product quality: what the product does, how it looks, the salesperson's attitude, the service person's knowledge, and the like. These characteristics are within the control of the organization that provided the product. The organization might not be able to control many things about its business environment, but it certainly can control the characteristics—or the quality—of its products.

The largest contributor to customer satisfaction, however, is something an organization can't fully control: the customer's perceptions. Whether they're based in fantasy, fiction, or some other state of unreality, perceptions have the weight of fact. In the business of pleasing customers, perceptions are fact.

Perceptions are also wildly inconsistent. Two different customers can consume the exact same product and have radically different perceptions about its quality. The differences may result from expectations each customer brought to the transaction, or they may simply result from varying powers of perception. Moreover, even one customer with consistent expectations might have varying perceptions about a product's quality, depending on his or her mood, or stress level, the time of day, the alignment of the planets—whatever. It's tempting to conclude that customer satisfaction is whatever the customer happens to think it is at any point in time.

Organizations interested in quantifying customer satisfaction must use data-gathering and analysis tools to better understand these elusive and ever-changing perceptions. They can then modify their products and operations to be more in sync with the market. Smart organizations employ a variety of tools to monitor customer satisfaction because no single tool is likely to capture the full range of information needed to truly understand perceptions.

Systems for gathering, understanding, and acting upon customer perceptions are among the most important an organization can implement. Organizations rarely view these systems as strategic initiatives, however; usually they're pushed so far down on the priority list that they become obscured and ignored. This is a fatal error, and one that's usually made at the top of an organization.

Business leaders must realize that pursuing customer satisfaction is a critical and strategic decision. It's not something an organization does simply to satisfy a standard or win an award: *It's something an organization does to stay in business.* Top management must embrace this reality by acknowledging, communicating, and acting upon three basic truths:

- ■ *Customer satisfaction is the ultimate goal.* There's no higher achievement than satisfying the customers an organization has committed itself to serving. This doesn't mean that the organization should abandon its competitive business sense and become a non-profit institution. Financial control is needed, along with accountability and sound decision making. But customer satisfaction is the ball everybody must keep his or her eyes on. Revenues and profits are nothing more than the results of fulfilling customer needs and expectations.
- ■ *Customer satisfaction is an investment.* This is important because customer satisfaction processes often don't produce results in the very short term. Payoffs more often are realized in the medium or long term. Resources must be applied to understanding customer requirements, collecting data on customer perceptions, and analyzing it. The resources required for these activities constitute one of the most important investments an organization can make, and this fact should be clearly reflected in budget planning.

■ *Everyone must be involved in customer satisfaction.* All personnel have the capability to influence customer satisfaction at some level. Top management must communicate exactly how personnel will be expected to contribute because it's often not intuitively obvious how this is possible. The following are real-life examples collected from organizations:

- Employees may spend as much as $2,000 to correct a deficiency or rectify a customer complaint (Ritz-Carlton Hotels).
- Employees must do everything possible to respond to customer requests before "sundown" on the day the requests are received (Wal-Mart).
- Customer care personnel, including the company president, are available to customers twenty-four hours a day (Texas Nameplate Co.).

The more employees understand their roles in customer satisfaction, the more they'll be able to participate. In the above examples, it's very clear what employees' roles are in driving customer satisfaction.

Top managers must set the tone for customer focus throughout the organization. They also ensure that adequate resources are applied to the effort. Once the appropriate cultural climate has been established and resources provided for understanding customer perceptions, it's time to begin gathering data.

This book presents five tools that can help organizations in this process. With one exception, the tools are all relatively easy to implement. Here's a quick overview of them:

■ *Call reports.* This is a simple method for using an existing customer communication system (e.g., telephone order, inquiry, or amendment) to probe customer perceptions. The dedication of time and resources for this tool is relatively low, and the burden on the customer is very light.

■ *Field reports.* This tool is typically implemented at the customer's location by means of the organization's representative, who explores issues more deeply than is possible during a call report. Because field reporting is conducted on-site with the customer, logistics and scheduling must be carefully planned in advance.

■ *Comment cards.* These simple tools provide a quick, convenient method for customer feedback. The information is usually timely, and service problems are promptly revealed. However, a system of comment cards requires daily management to be effective.

■ *Complaint systems.* Despite the seemingly defensive nature of this system, complaints can be channeled into positive experiences if the organization responds properly. Chapter 5 contains examples of tools and protocols needed to respond effectively to complaints and restore customer satisfaction—and maybe even enhance it.

■ *Quantitative customer surveys.* These are relatively complex tools designed to build an understanding of what customers think about an organization's performance. Quantitative customer surveys include questions and/or statements relating to performance, each followed by a scale the customer uses to record his or her perceptions. Because of their complexity, these surveys aren't generally recommended for an organization's first foray into gauging customer satisfaction.

Every organization must develop a strategy for becoming more connected to marketplace perceptions. Wisely using the tools described in the following chapters will assist in this pursuit. While reading, keep in mind that it's not enough to simply understand customer perceptions. Organizations must act on perceptions, day in and day out. This is the only path to securing long-term success.

Now let's take a closer look at the individual tools. Think about what will work best in your own organization, and don't hesitate to customize the tools and guidelines where it makes sense to do so.

Chapter 2

Call
Reports

Call reports are an especially simple and user-friendly way to capture information about customer perceptions. The concept is basic: Spend a few extra minutes during an existing customer interaction, usually while taking an order or answering a question over the telephone, to ask a few questions. If the questions are meaningful, then your organization leverages an existing event to learn more about what the customer really thinks about your goods and/or services. The benefits of a call report are obvious:

■ *Proactive interest.* You're reaching out to the customer, instead of the other way around.

■ *Brevity.* Call reports require only a few minutes to perform. This respects the customer's time and minimizes the time spent by people within your organization.

■ *Unobtrusiveness.* There are no forms for the customer to interpret and complete.

■ *Candor.* Usually there's an existing rapport between the person performing the call report and the customer representative. The answers will probably be more honest because of this relationship.

■ *Low cost.* Call reports take only a few minutes of somebody's time. The individual performing the call report is typically a customer service rep, someone who already spends a significant portion of his or her time talking to customers.

■ *Simplicity.* Anybody can perform a call report after receiving appropriate training. It doesn't require outside expertise to implement.

5

■ *Versatility.* Call reports will work with just about any customer: manufacturer, authorized dealer, reseller, or final consumer. They can also be performed for a tangible good, a pure service, or both.

Despite the wide range of benefits, however, call reports aren't perfect tools. The results depend very much on the manner in which the tool is administered. For this reason, training is crucial before the first call report is attempted. Training issues are addressed under "Dos and don'ts of call reports" later in this chapter. Make sure all personnel have received training on—and fully understand—the dos and don'ts.

Another potential drawback is the open-ended nature of the questions. I consider open-ended questions a positive attribute because they allow the customer representative to elaborate and provide whatever details he or she feels are important. Many people hold the opposing view, however. Open-ended responses aren't scaled, and this makes traditional statistical analysis difficult. Lack of scaling also complicates comparing results from one year to the next.

Possibly the biggest drawback to call reports is that the person being interviewed typically doesn't use the product in question. This is particularly true in an industrial environment where, more often than not, the interviewee is a purchasing agent or office manager, someone who is one or two steps removed from firsthand information about the product in question. Sure, you'll get some feedback about your product, but that feedback's timeliness and accuracy may be questionable. For this reason, a special tool is needed to reach deeper into the customer's organization and solicit insights from the people who work directly with the product you supply.

TWO-STAGE CALL REPORTS

The two-stage call report (shown at the end of this chapter) is designed to delve deeper into the customer's organization by not only querying the purchasing agent or office manager, but also the actual product user. Stage one of the call report is performed with the initial customer contact via telephone. As mentioned earlier, this is done during an existing customer interaction such as while placing an order, making an inquiry, or requesting a quote. After the call's primary purpose has been addressed, the employee mentions that he or she would like to ask a few questions that won't take more than a few minutes. Three questions about the organization's goods and/or services are then asked:

■ *Is there anything about our products or services that you haven't complained about, but which you find to be less than satisfactory?* This question probes for possible problems that may be brewing but that the customer hasn't told you about. Remember, only a fraction of all complaints are actually reported. Here, you're trying to increase your percentage of reported complaints. Being proactive is the key.

■ *Is there anything that we've done particularly well lately?* Surprisingly, organizations often please their customers through informal, accidental, or unrecognized actions. These little pockets of "wow!" often go unrepeated. You want to understand these actions and make them systematic, but they can't become systematic unless they're known.

Don't push too hard with this question, however. It's possible that your organization has done nothing particularly well lately. If the customer has a "no" response, then move on to the next question. Don't persist until you become embarrassed, and the customer becomes irritated.

■ *What could we do that would make your job easier or help make you more successful?* This question attempts to look into the future and find out what should be done to improve the product. Any aspect of the product is game here: the ordering process, product literature or information, packaging or labeling, delivery, additional desired features, or functionality.

The customer representative's responses are recorded after each question. Two final questions are then asked: "Who else in your organization uses our products?" and "Do you mind providing their contact information so that we can ask them the same questions?" This is your opportunity to find the true product users. They could be almost anyone. The users' level within the organization doesn't matter; what does is that they have direct experience using your product. If the customer representative is reluctant to provide this additional contact information, carefully explaining the reason for it—a desire to improve your overall performance and the customer's success—should help. The customer representative is then thanked for his or her valuable time.

Stage two of the call report is executed by contacting the product user you've just identified. This should be done immediately to prevent the product user from being "coached" on the questions and before you forget.

The same three questions are asked during stage two. Be patient because the person you're speaking with may not have experience answering these kinds of questions. He or she might be downright uncomfortable about it. A friendly voice and forthright manner are the two best techniques for putting someone at ease. Remember to mention that the purpose of the interview is to identify ways that your organization can become a better supplier and make that person's job easier.

SAMPLING CUSTOMERS: WHO, WHEN, AND WHY?

Once the organization decides to conduct call reports, it must determine its rationale for sampling customers. There are no absolutes to how often call reports should be done and which customers should be sampled. It's more important to experiment with an approach and then be prepared to change if it appears to be ineffective. The ultimate objective is to understand your customers' perceptions and use this information to improve your performance. There are a number of different approaches to reach this objective. The two most typical sampling schemes are as follows:

■ *Time.* Many organizations elect to sample their customers at regular intervals, such as quarterly, biannually, or annually. This may be the easiest method because the only planning required is scheduling with the appropriate personnel. The drawback is that it treats all customers the same, with minor customers being sampled as often as major ones.

■ *Importance.* Another tactic is to sample customers based on their relative importance to your organization's success. The most typically "important" factors include sales revenues, average profit margin, frequency of orders, and potential for future business. Using this method, you might sample those customers who place frequent orders more often than you will the infrequent customers. Also, customers with whom you'd like to do more business might be sampled more frequently than low-margin, high-maintenance customers. This tactic requires a bit more planning and research, but the additional work pays off in the form of information slanted in the direction your organization is moving.

It's worth noting that neither of these sampling methodologies are statistically valid. In other words, you won't be able to draw conclusions about the universe of customer perceptions based upon the results of the sample. You certainly can identify opportunities for increasing customer satisfaction, however. A discussion of statistically valid sampling techniques is included in chapter 6.

DOS AND DON'TS OF CALL REPORTS

A number of fundamental dos and don'ts should be considered when conducting call reports. These should be included when implementing any call reporting system:

✔ *Do record the results using a structured form.* Relying on your memory or informal notes as a record of what was said during a call report will ultimately prove a waste of time and effort. Develop a form in accordance with your organization's method of doing business. (See the form at the end of this chapter for an example.)

✔ *Do provide practice opportunities.* Performing a scripted interview isn't something that comes naturally to most people. Without practice, you may come across as stiff and unnatural, and the customer's responses will be stiff and unnatural as well. All personnel who will be performing call reports should have opportunities to practice before their first attempt. Use co-workers to practice on and ask for honest feedback. It may be useful to record practice sessions so they can hear how they sound on the other end of the phone. When all personnel feel comfortable using this tool—and confident in their ability to capture perceptions with it—you're ready to implement call reports.

✔ *Do assign someone to be in charge.* A team typically performs call reports, with each person calling his or her own customers. Make sure that someone in a position of authority has been assigned the role of call report supervisor. Otherwise, call reports might not happen according to plan.

✔ *Do prepare beforehand.* Research your company's history with the customer before a call report is performed. If there are open complaints that haven't been addressed yet, hold off on the call. The customer will be justifiably irritated that you're asking about perceptions when you've already been told about one of them. When complaints do occur, be prepared to notify the customer of your progress in remedying the situation. Call reports should be performed only when there are no open complaints or when the customer has already been notified of your progress in addressing an existing complaint.

✔ *Do sample existing customers.* The two-stage call report at the end of this chapter is designed for use with existing customers. The questions couldn't be answered reasonably by anyone else. For this reason, sample only existing customers when using this tool. You'll need to use a different approach when sampling prospective customers.

✔ *Do ask permission.* Make sure to indicate your intentions of performing a call report and ask if the customer has a problem with this. If you've explained that it will take only a few minutes, most customers will readily agree. This is nothing more than a basic courtesy.

✔ *Do listen actively.* Focus on the responses you receive to your questions. Make sure you understand what's being said. If you don't, clarify the response with the customer. It may be necessary to rephrase the question. When you understand what's being said, provide verbal cues that you are hearing and comprehending the information. Simple verbal cues such as, "Yes, I understand" and "OK, sure" let customers know they're being heard. The responses will be more meaningful when customers think they're being heard and understood. Remember, you can't be seen over a telephone, so it's important to verbally acknowledge understanding.

✔ *Do thank the interviewee.* End the call report by thanking the customer for his or her time. Be honest in your appreciation of his or her input and candor. This will usually ensure the customer's willingness to do it again in the future.

✗ *Don't sample too often.* Pestering customers by performing call reports too frequently is counterproductive. Sampling more frequently than once a quarter is probably a mistake because it will take at least three months to understand and take action on what you've already sampled. It makes no sense to capture additional information until you've acted on existing information.

✗ *Don't perform a call report during a complaint call.* When a customer calls to complain, don't ask for feedback about the product. Dedicate all your time and attention to the complaint at hand. The customer will think that you're minimizing his or her complaint's importance if you attempt to wedge a call report into the conversation.

✗ *Don't debate the issues.* Remember, the call report is all about customer perceptions. If the customer perceives something, it has the weight of fact. Don't try to argue or debate with the customer about the facts. Simply record the customer's perceptions, and thank him or her.

✗ *Don't make promises you can't keep.* Occasionally, it's tempting to respond to what you learn during a call report by making outrageous promises. "I can guarantee you'll see a significant improvement in our delivery performance!" Although something like this sounds quite good, don't say it unless your organization can back it up with results. Making empty promises is a sure way to plunge customer satisfaction into the negative zone.

✗ *Don't interrupt the interviewee.* Some customers may want to vent. This call report may be the opportunity they've been waiting for. Although it's tempting to cut them off, don't do it. Let the customers work out whatever is on their mind. Record as much as possible, and edit irrelevant information later.

✗ *Don't get distracted.* Concentrate on talking to the customer. Don't allow your mind to wander or the call report will be worthless. Stay focused on the issues by making a mental picture of what's being discussed.

ANALYSIS AND ACTION

Analyzing data from call reports is quite simple if you:

■ *Review the results of each call report.* Urgent issues should be forwarded immediately to the complaint system.

■ *Periodically analyze call reports performed during a given period.* Usually this will involve consolidating and summarizing the customers' perceptions into the three categories suggested by the call report questions: unreported problems, things you're doing well, and enhancements and improvements. Common themes will emerge across multiple reports. These form the basis for action. Spreadsheet software such as Lotus 1-2-3 or Excel can facilitate this kind of analysis. An example of this follows:

	A	B	C	D
1	Categorization of Issues—Call Reports from January–March 2003			
2	Call Report No.	Unreported Problems	Things We're Doing Well	Desired Improvements
3	03-001	None	None	Would like better packaging —wrapping often dirty
4	03-002	Last shipment had mud and grease on exterior packaging	Fast service—thanks!	Work on appearance of product arrival
5	03-003	Invoice 22327 had wrong price for style J widgets. It was fixed by A/R department.		
6	03-004	Dirty wrapping on last two shipments	Quick turnaround time	Wish products showed up looking a little better

■ *Discuss the common themes in a group setting.* The group will prioritize them and pick one to address. There's no right way to do this. Typically, it comes down to the group's collective experience and management's guidance.

■ *Brainstorm actions that will affect the theme the group has agreed to address.* The actions can be prioritized by using a system of multivoting or through a more quantitative method. With multivoting, participants are given three to five votes each for "voting" on the idea they believe to be the most effective. They can place all of their votes on one action or spread them around. The results determine which action will be pursued. Multivoting is a good selection system to use when all participants understand equally the issues at hand and group buy-in is critical.

■ *Enter chosen actions into the corrective or preventive action system.* This will ensure some degree of project planning and closure.

■ *Tell customers when you've made improvements and/or corrections.* Let them know that the impetus for taking the action was the information gained during a call report. Customers will realize that the time spent answering call report questions is a good investment.

Call reports are a relatively easy way to gather information on customer perceptions. They can be used to great advantage not only by organizations just beginning to gather customer perceptions, but also by those that are familiar with the process and are looking for one more way to track customer satisfaction.

A sample two-stage call report form is shown on the following two pages.

Call Report No. _____

TWO-STAGE CALL REPORT—STAGE ONE

(To be performed while on the phone with the customer representative)

Performed By: _____	Date: ____/____/____ Time: _____
Company Name: _____	Location: _____
Contact Name: _____	Title: _____
Phone Number: _____	E-mail: _____

While I've got you on the phone, do you mind if I ask you a few quick questions? It won't take more than a couple of minutes.

1. Is there anything about our products or services that you find to be less than satisfactory that you haven't previously brought to our attention?	
Comments: _____	**Yes ❏ No ❏**
_____	

2. Is there anything that we've done particularly well lately?	
Comments: _____	**Yes ❏ No ❏**
_____	

3. What could we do to make your job easier or make you more successful?
Comments: _____
_____

4. Is there anyone else in your organization who uses our products? Would you mind providing their name and number so that we may contact them?	
Name: _____	Title: _____
Phone Number: _____	E-mail: _____

Thank you very much for your time. It's a pleasure doing business with you.

Call Report No. _____

TWO-STAGE CALL REPORT—STAGE TWO

(To be performed after you've identified the product user)

Performed By: _____	Date: ___/___/___ Time: _____

Hello. This is _____ from_____. As you probably know, we supply you with_____. Do you mind if I ask you a few quick questions? It won't take more than a couple of minutes.

1. How do you use our products and services?

_____

_____

_____

2. Is there anything about our products or services that you find to be less than satisfactory that you haven't previously brought to our attention?

Comments: _____	Yes ❑ No ❑

3. Is there anything that we've done particularly well lately?

Comments: _____	Yes ❑ No ❑

4. What could we do that would make your job easier or help make you more successful?

Comments: _____

_____

Call report reviewed by: _____	Date: ___/___/___

Thank you very much for your time. It's a pleasure doing business with you.

Chapter 3

Field
Reports

In This Chapter
- Field reporting tools
- Implementation procedures
- Dos and don'ts of field reports
- Industrial, service, and dealer field report forms

T he most basic definition of a field report is a study performed outside your organization. A representative from your organization goes to where your product is being sold, demonstrated, installed, processed, or consumed, and gathers firsthand information about customer perceptions. Field reports might be performed when:

■ A salesperson makes a routine visit to a customer.

■ Company representatives visit an authorized dealer or retail location to discuss marketing issues.

■ A team of employees visit a customer to better understand processing issues.

■ Technical or repair personnel make troubleshooting visits to a customer.

■ A product specialist interacts with consumers at the point of product delivery.

■ Anyone within the organization makes a special visit for the express purpose of performing a field report.

During the visit, customer perceptions are explored and recorded, usually by means of a structured form. An on-site company representative can gather perceptions from the customer first-hand. The benefits of this type of interview are significant:

■ The representative can observe the product being used and learn of unstated customer requirements and expectations.

15

- Responses to questions are ensured because the customer representative is right there with the customer.
- The appropriate person for each type of question can usually be located. Thus you can talk to the production supervisor about processing issues, the warehouse coordinator about packaging issues, and the accounts payable clerk about billing issues.
- The field report doesn't require additional time to perform because it can usually be added to a scheduled visit to the customer.
- When performed correctly, field reports send a powerful message to the customer that your organization is focused on their needs and expectations. You've reached out to them in person to find out how you can become a better partner.

One of the negatives related to field reports is their cost. Travel to customer locations usually incurs significant expense. Smart organizations will be selective about which customers are chosen for field reports. Although all customers might be sampled for a round of call reports, only a select number might be sampled for field reports. These reports are performed when you already have a reason to be on-site with the customer so the visit serves double duty.

Another potential drawback is the way the field reporting system is structured. In some organizations, they aren't structured at all. The format, content, protocols, and timing are left strictly up to the employees operating in the field. This is a huge mistake. Don't squander the opportunity of understanding customer perceptions by approaching the task in a haphazard manner. Carefully design all aspects of the field reporting process, document the system, and then make certain that all employees involved in field reporting understand how they fit into the system. Leaving decisions up to individuals will ensure variation and provide little informational value.

FIELD REPORTING TOOLS

Three basic tools are relevant to field reporting. In essence, field report tools are concise customer surveys that are administered in person at the customer's location. They might differ in terms of the subjects that are probed, but their formats are generally similar to one another. They include:

- *Industrial field reports.* Designed for organizations that provide a tangible product to industrial customers who then process or assemble the product into an intermediate or finished product. The form attempts to capture a range of issues relevant to successfully serving this type of account.
- *Dealer field reports.* Designed for organizations that supply a finished product to an authorized dealer or retail location, which then resells the product to the final consumer. The questions attempt to probe issues on dual fronts: the quality of the product

experience from the dealer's or store's viewpoint, and the quality of the product experience from the final consumer's standpoint.

■ *Service field reports.* Designed for organizations whose primary product is a service. Because there's no tangible product to evaluate, issues related to timing, communication, and professionalism are highlighted with this method.

The tools differ by only a question or two each. Strong arguments could be made for or against each of the issues addressed. The tools themselves can certainly be used as is but would be even stronger if customized to the organization based on the product attributes that are most critical to driving customer satisfaction. It's best to keep the field report as short as possible—you can wear out your welcome if the exercise becomes too time consuming.

Depending on how the responses are solicited, field reporting tools can be designed with either scaled or open-ended responses. Scaled responses have the advantage of producing a numerical score that can easily be tracked and compared over time. Scores appeal to many data-driven organizations that are accustomed to measuring nearly everything they do. A purely scaled response, however, doesn't give customers an opportunity to elaborate on issues they believe are important. An open-ended structure allows them to provide whatever feedback they feel is relevant. Possibly the best design is a hybrid that incorporates both scaled and open-ended responses. The examples shown in the documents at the end of this chapter use a hybrid approach. Scaling is explained in more detail in chapter 6.

Besides merely collecting information on customer perceptions, a field report should be an opportunity for the organization's representatives to collect their own perceptions. You're there at the customer's location—why not take a look around? Specifically, your organization's representative should be attuned to any of the following situations:

■ Unintended product applications
■ Possible product misuse
■ Damage to the product, regardless of how, when, or who causes it
■ Product defects
■ Evidence of deterioration
■ Packaging or labeling problems
■ Comments of people using the product
■ Apparent frustration of people using the product

With prior approval, take photos of your product as it appears at the customer site. Photos convey graphic information that can greatly enhance customers' comments. They also have a significant impact on the people back at your own facility. Just make sure you don't photograph confidential portions of the customer's site.

IMPLEMENTATION PROCEDURES

There are many ways to go about implementing a system of field reports, but here's a common-sense approach that works for most organizations:

- Take advantage of already scheduled visits to customers for field reports.
- Establish protocols, responsibilities, and authorities for performing field reports and analyzing data. These system details should be incorporated into a documented procedure.
- Educate everyone on the system. Impress upon the participants the importance of capturing clear and accurate customer perceptions—as well as their own perceptions—by using the field reporting process.
- Develop a preliminary schedule for performing field reports.
- Contact customers to verify acceptance of preliminary schedule.
- Finalize the schedule and communicate it to all parties involved.
- Carry out field reports, capturing as much information possible.
- Use what you learn to drive continual improvement of the product.

DOS AND DON'TS OF FIELD REPORTS

The following considerations should be kept in mind when implementing a system of field reports. You might want to brainstorm additional dos and don'ts that are customized to your industry or style of doing business. Incorporate these into the procedure you develop to guide the field reporting process.

- ✔ *Do locate the right person to answer each question.* Except in smaller organizations, different questions most likely will need to be addressed by different people. This will introduce logistical challenges to the field reporting process but will significantly increase the information's value.

- ✔ *Do get specifics.* Generalities are almost worthless from the standpoint of customer perceptions. Press for specific details related to good and bad experiences with your product. If possible, inspect the issues firsthand so you can see for yourself. Record details such as product identification, batch numbers, serial numbers, dates, service person names, and exact nature of problems and/or virtues. Keep in mind that your organization must act on the data collected, and vague statements are very difficult to act upon. The more specific the feedback, the better.

- ✔ *Do take photos after getting permission from the customer.* One of the biggest benefits of field reports is that you can actually see what the product looks like and how it performs. The best way to communicate what you see is through photos. Digital cameras are especially suited to this task because the results can be viewed and e-mailed immediately.

- ✔ *Do share your notes with the customer.* You'll probably be taking notes in the presence of the customer representative, which might arouse curiosity and/or suspicion. To diffuse any conflicts, always offer to share your notes with the customer. The whole process is about becoming a better business partner, and there's nothing confidential about that.

✔ *Do maintain professionalism when discussing competitors' products.* Part of any field report is asking for comparisons between your products and those of your competitors. This is perfectly acceptable, but be careful to maintain a level of professionalism. Your words and actions should be the same as if your competitor were standing beside you.

✘ *Don't pass judgment on what you see and hear.* It may be tempting to perform root-cause analysis on the spot during a field report. After all, you're examining firsthand perceptions, and you may even be looking at the product itself. Gather information and pass judgment on the issue later, when you have the time to analyze all the variables and their interactions.

✘ *Don't get distracted.* It's easy to become sidetracked by long lunches, golf outings, conversations, and other diversions. Use the field report form to help you stay focused and on schedule.

✘ *Don't limit yourself strictly to the issues on the field report.* Just because an issue is not addressed on the field reporting form doesn't mean you can't pursue it. Remember, field reports' ultimate objectives are to improve your products and become a better business partner. Any information that might lead to this objective should be recorded. Make sure to revise the field report by adding, deleting, or editing questions as circumstances evolve.

✘ *Don't influence or steer the responses.* Your offhand remarks, body language, facial expressions, and tone of voice can influence the way someone responds to a question. Try to present each question in a neutral, even manner.

ANALYSIS AND ACTION

The process for analyzing field report data is very similar to the one used for call reports.

■ *The person performing the field report should review the responses for issues that need immediate investigation and action.* These should be communicated back to the organization via phone, fax, or e-mail—whichever is fastest. Urgent problems are converted directly into complaints. Assure the customer that the issue is receiving immediate attention.

■ *Periodically summarize the results of the field reports performed during a given period.* Scaled responses should be tabulated and averaged, and open-ended responses compiled by question. Common themes will emerge across multiple reports. These—and significant outliers—form the basis for action. Conversion of data to simple graphics can assist in the interpretation of issues. An example of this is shown on the next page.

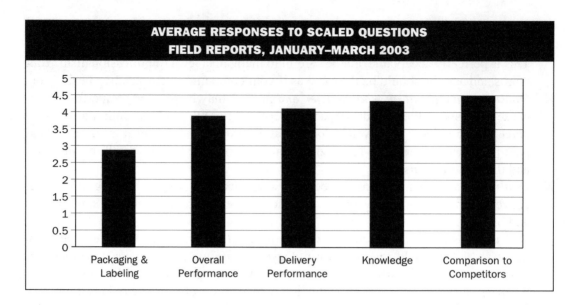

- *Discuss the common themes and significant outliers in a group setting.* The group will prioritize the issues and pick one to address. There's no right way to prioritize the themes. Typically, it will come down to the group's collective experience and management's guidance. Often, the most significant issues stand out during graphic analysis of data, so there's less need for debate on actions needed.
- *Brainstorm actions that will affect the theme the group has agreed to address.* These can be prioritized by using a system of multivoting or a more quantitative method.
- *Input actions into the corrective or preventive action system.* This will ensure some degree of project planning and closure. More complex actions might require a formal project plan to guide their progress.
- *Tell customers when you've made an improvement and/or correction.* Let them know that the impetus for taking the action was the information gained during a field report. They'll realize that the time spent answering field report questions is a good investment on their part.

Field reports provide a significant amount of informational value in a user-friendly approach. Perhaps the biggest benefit is that the organization gets to see and hear firsthand how its customers perceive the products they buy. A system of field reporting is the perfect tool for organizations that want to strike a balance between a complex procedure and valuable information.

Sample industrial, service, and dealer field report forms are shown on the following pages.

INDUSTRIAL FIELD REPORT

Performed By: _____	Date: ___/___/___ Time: _____
Company Name: _____	Division: _____
Address: _____	
Products Supplied: _____	
Contact Name: _____	Title: _____
Phone Number: _____	E-mail: _____
Purpose of Visit: _____	

Ask the applicable customer representative how we're doing in each of the categories below. Remind the customer to be honest in his or her responses—being nice won't help either of us in the long run.

1. How would you describe the overall performance of our products?

❑ **1** Very Poor	❑ **2** Poor	❑ **3** Adequate	❑ **4** Good	❑ **5** Very Good

What's something specific we could improve upon in this category? _____
_____

2. Please rate our ability to meet delivery dates.

❑ **1** Very Poor	❑ **2** Poor	❑ **3** Adequate	❑ **4** Good	❑ **5** Very Good

What's something specific we could improve upon in this category? _____
_____

3. How would you describe the packaging and labeling of our products?

❑ **1** Very Poor	❑ **2** Poor	❑ **3** Adequate	❑ **4** Good	❑ **5** Very Good

What's something specific we could improve upon in this category? _____
_____

Field Report No. _____

4. How would you rate the knowledge and courtesy of our personnel?

❏ **1** Very Poor	❏ **2** Poor	❏ **3** Adequate	❏ **4** Good	❏ **5** Very Good

What's something specific we could improve upon in this category? _____
_____

5. How do our products compare to our competitors' products?

❏ **1** Far Worse	❏ **2** Worse	❏ **3** About the Same	❏ **4** Better	❏ **5** Much Better

Can you provide some specific details related to how we compare? _____
_____

6. Do you have any complaints or problems related to our products that you haven't told us about?

_____

7. What are our products' biggest strengths?

_____

8. What do you see as our products' most significant weaknesses?

_____

9. What would you like to see us do differently or better in the future?

_____

Contact for This Field Report: _____	Phone: _____
Field Report Reviewed By: _____	Date: ____/____/____
Resulting Actions: _____	

Field Report No. _____

SERVICE FIELD REPORT

Performed By: _____	Date: ___/___/___ Time: _____
Customer Name: _____	Address: _____
Services Provided to Them: _____	
Contact Name: _____	Title: _____
Phone Number: _____	E-mail: _____
Purpose of Visit: _____	

Ask the applicable customer representative how we're doing in each of the categories below. Remind the customer to be honest in his or her responses—being nice won't help either of us in the long run.

1. Rate our accessibility when you need to contact us:

❏ **1** Very Poor	❏ **2** Poor	❏ **3** Adequate	❏ **4** Good	❏ **5** Very Good

What's something specific we could improve upon in this category? _____

2. How would you describe our responsiveness to your needs?

❏ **1** Very Poor	❏ **2** Poor	❏ **3** Adequate	❏ **4** Good	❏ **5** Very Good

What's something specific we could improve upon in this category? _____

3. How would you rate our ability to complete work within the time promised?

❏ **1** Very Poor	❏ **2** Poor	❏ **3** Adequate	❏ **4** Good	❏ **5** Very Good

What's something specific we could improve upon in this category? _____

4. How would you rate the effectiveness of our services?

❏ **1** Very Poor	❏ **2** Poor	❏ **3** Adequate	❏ **4** Good	❏ **5** Very Good

What's something specific we could improve upon in this category? _____

Field Report No. _____

4. How would you rate the knowledge and courtesy of our personnel?

❑ **1** Very Poor	❑ **2** Poor	❑ **3** Adequate	❑ **4** Good	❑ **5** Very Good

What's something specific we could improve upon in this category? _____
_____

5. How do our products compare to our competitors' products?

❑ **1** Far Worse	❑ **2** Worse	❑ **3** About the Same	❑ **4** Better	❑ **5** Much Better

Can you provide some specific details related to how we compare? _____
_____

6. Do you have any complaints or problems related to our products that you haven't told us about?
_____
_____

7. What are our products' biggest strengths?
_____
_____

8. What do you see as our products' most significant weaknesses?
_____
_____

9. What would you like to see us do differently or better in the future?
_____
_____

Contact for This Field Report: _____	Phone: _____
Field Report Reviewed By: _____	Date: ___/___/___
Resulting Actions: _____	

Field Report No. _____

DEALER FIELD REPORT

Performed By: _____	Date: ___/___/___ Time: _____
Dealer/Store Name: _____	Address: _____
Products Supplied: _____	
Contact Name: _____	Title: _____
Phone Number: _____	E-mail: _____
Purpose of Visit: _____	

Ask the applicable customer representative how we're doing in each of the categories below. Remind the customer to be honest in his or her responses—being nice won't help either of us in the long run.

1. How would you rate the condition of our products upon arrival at your location?

❏ **1** Very Poor	❏ **2** Poor	❏ **3** Adequate	❏ **4** Good	❏ **5** Very Good

What's something specific we could improve upon in this category? _____

2. How would you rate the attractiveness of our products and their ability to "stand out from the crowd"?

❏ **1** Very Poor	❏ **2** Poor	❏ **3** Adequate	❏ **4** Good	❏ **5** Very Good

What's something specific we could improve upon in this category? _____

3. How would you describe the overall performance of our products?

❏ **1** Very Poor	❏ **2** Poor	❏ **3** Adequate	❏ **4** Good	❏ **5** Very Good

What's something specific we could improve upon in this category? _____

4. How do our products compare to our competitors' products?

❏ **1** Far Worse	❏ **2** Worse	❏ **3** About the Same	❏ **4** Better	❏ **5** Much Better

Can you provide some specific details related to how we compare? _____

Field Report No. _____

5. Based on what you've heard and seen lately, what issues seem to be most important to the final consumer?

Can you provide some specific details related to how we compare?_____

_____

6. Do you have any complaints or problems related to our products that you haven't told us about?

_____

_____

7. What are our products' biggest strengths?

_____

_____

8. What do you see as our products' most significant weaknesses?

_____

_____

9. What would you like to see us do differently or better in the future?

_____

_____

Contact for This Field Report: _____   Phone: _____

Field Report Reviewed By: _____   Date: ___/___/___

Resulting Actions: _____

_____

Chapter 4

Comment Cards

Comment cards can be found almost everywhere. These compact tools, usually not much larger than index cards, pop up in a broad range of business contexts. The use of comment cards is so widespread, in fact, that many people, customers and employees alike, consider them to be nothing more than a nuisance. This is unfortunate because they have the potential to provide timely, useful feedback. Here are some of the locations where comment cards can be found, along with the type of feedback they capture:

- *Restaurants.* Cards are located on dining tables or near registers. Questions concern the quality of food, efficiency of service, and courtesy of personnel.
- *Hotels.* Cards are located at or near the check-in desk or in guest rooms. Questions relate to the courtesy of personnel, cleanliness of rooms, ease of reservations, and check-in.
- *Consumer products.* Cards are usually included with user manuals and warranties. Questions relate to the product's performance, clarity of instructions, and inclusion of all necessary components.
- *Industrial products.* Cards are usually included with packing lists or instructional materials. Questions concern the product's condition upon arrival, timeliness of delivery, and product performance.

- *Theme parks and cruises.* Cards are carried by service people or are available in administrative areas. Questions deal with the courtesy and helpfulness of personnel and convenience of facilities.
- *Repair or technical services.* Cards are occasionally carried by service people. Questions relate to the timeliness and effectiveness of the service as well as the courtesy of personnel.
- *Governmental services.* Cards are occasionally offered where governmental services are performed. Questions have to do with the range of services, adequacy of facilities, and courtesy of personnel.

Keep in mind that, despite their names, comment cards can take almost any form: a card, a small form, the reverse side of a packing list, an Internet Web site, or an e-mail. It's important that they're brief enough to be completed in a couple of minutes. A comment card shouldn't cover too many topics, and it shouldn't appear intimidating to the customer. You're relying on your customers to take the time to provide you with feedback, so don't overburden them with too big of a task. A comment card shouldn't resemble a full-blown customer survey that's simply been shrunk in size.

One of the drawbacks of comment cards is that they tend to capture very general comments. This is a function of their size as well as what, to customers, constitutes a "comment." It's also a function of the amount of time customers are willing to invest in completing a card—usually not much. These facts aside, general comments such as, "I had trouble assembling the bicycle," or "Dinner wasn't as good as in the past," don't provide much guidance for making improvements. Make it clear to your customers that you need specific details. Some organizations won't accept comment cards without specific details or that aren't completely filled out, although this seems a bit arrogant. A much better tactic would be to educate customers on the type of information needed. A simple message printed directly on the card itself, such as, "Please provide specific details of your experience (the who, what, where, and when) so we can make improvements," should suffice.

Comment cards also tend to capture feedback extremes, either very good or very bad experiences. After all, these extremes are what motivate customers to offer feedback in the first place. This drawback requires recognition more than action. It's doubtful that customers can be motivated to provide feedback on every kind of transaction. Organizations that use this tool must realize that the feedback won't provide a balanced picture of their performance; it will be skewed.

Once a comment card is completed, the customer needs a way to get it back to your organization. The method for returning cards must be carefully considered. Asking people to return them to service people is generally a bad idea because cards tend to disappear when they include negative feedback. A better method would be a secured receptacle—a locked box, for instance—where cards can be returned, or affixing postage to the cards so they can be dropped directly into the mail. Or provide a computer terminal where comments can be typed in and transmitted. A growing number of organizations provide a feedback link from their Web pages, and this serves as an electronic comment card. (Search the Internet using the term "comment card" to see how widespread electronic comment cards have become.)

Electronic comment cards have a number of advantages over hard-copy varieties:

- Information arrives instantaneously. There's no response delay due to mail or storage.
- Feedback can be transferred automatically into a database for trend analysis and record keeping. There's no chance of a transcription error.
- Long-term costs are lower once the system is established (although the up-front costs are most certainly higher).
- Electronic tools are convenient. They're ready and available whenever the customer is. No paper cards to maintain.

One caution: Not all customers are equally comfortable using electronic or Web-based tools. Provide hard-copy alternatives for these customers.

When acted upon, comment cards can generate significant customer loyalty. Many organizations provide free meals, free hotel stays, or discounts on future purchases to individuals who submit negative feedback on comment cards. These "freebies" can generate significant goodwill, provided one condition is met: The compensation is paired with an improvement over the bad experience. The message to the customer needs to be, "Not only will you receive a free night's stay in our hotel, but we'll do everything in our power to remedy the situation that you told us about." The customer actually receives two things: a freebie and a fix. A fix without a freebie is fine, but a freebie without a fix is worthless.

QUESTIONABLE USES OF COMMENT CARDS

Organizations often use comment cards for reasons other than collecting customer feedback. Their intentions become obvious when customers are asked for their postal address, favorite pastimes, highest level of education, or household income. The true purpose of these cards is to build marketing databases and even to sell demographic information to other organizations.

Using comment cards for any reason other than gathering customer feedback is a deceptive practice and should be avoided. Customers aren't so naïve as to misunderstand the intentions of these disguised tools, and they will be shunned. The only contact information that should appear on a comment card is the customer's name and phone number or e-mail address, and these should be used only to clarify the feedback or to communicate improvements and/or an offer of compensation.

If the organization wants to collect contact information on customers for advertising purposes, it should do so in a different way. One method is to ask customers to put their business cards into a fish bowl for the chance of winning a free lunch. Once a week, a business card is drawn for the free lunch, and the remaining cards are entered into the advertising database. This ensures that the comment card process remains purely about feedback and provides a different avenue for collecting contact information for marketing and advertising purposes. Still somewhat deceptive? Maybe. But at least the credibility of the comment card process hasn't been weakened.

Another questionable application of comment cards is for rewarding employees who receive positive feedback. This is prevalent in the travel industry. You may wonder why this would be a questionable application. After all, the organization is only trying to reward the people who perform well. True, but when rewards become established, the focus of the comment cards process can quickly become about rewards, not about improving as an organization. In some companies, employees are tempted to instruct customers about the "correct" way to complete the comment cards (i.e., check only the boxes marked "Excellent").

If the organization wants to reward employees for performance, then employees must be advised not to coach customers on how to fill out the cards. Customers don't like to be told what feedback to provide, and receiving only positive feedback all the time—especially when it's the result of coaching—doesn't help the organization make improvements. Organizations should proceed cautiously if rewards are attached to the comment card process, otherwise the whole system could turn into a waste of time.

IMPLEMENTATION PROCEDURES

Implementing a comment card process requires a significant amount of planning. This might sound counterintuitive for such a simple tool, but planning is needed because comment cards, like surveys, must be self-explanatory. Here are some general steps to take when implementing a system of comment cards:

- ■ *Benchmark existing comment cards in your own industry.* Search for examples on the Internet.
- ■ *Decide on the best medium for your comment cards.* These can include cards, forms, Web pages, or a combination of all three.
- ■ *Decide whether you'll employ an open-ended format or one that asks for specific at-*

tributes. If you go with specific questions, brainstorm a short list of critical attributes. Refer to the comment card examples at the end of this chapter.

■ *Design a draft comment card tool.* Get feedback from trusted customers on its content and usefulness. Improve the tool based on the feedback you receive.

■ *Develop procedures for administering the comment card system.* This will include how the cards will be made available to customers, how they'll be returned, who will be responsible for reviewing them and taking action, and who will follow-up with customers.

■ *Train all employees on their role within the comment card system.* Emphasize that coaching customers is counterproductive.

■ *Communicate to customers how important their feedback is.* Let them know that an easy way to share their feedback is through your comment card system. This communication can be done verbally or through written instruction. But don't push the system too much. It's always the customer's choice to fill out the comment card or not.

■ *Manage the system.* Investigate the issues revealed on comment cards as quickly as possible, and tell customers about corrective actions whenever possible. Always thank customers for their feedback.

■ *Examine trends in comment card feedback.* You might be surprised by what you learn.

DOS AND DON'TS OF COMMENT CARDS

Following are some of the essential dos and don'ts related to managing a system of comment cards. Most of these guidelines have been touched upon already, but they're important to review and explicitly incorporate into your process:

✔ *Do keep the card very short and simple.* Remember, you're relying on customers to fill these things out. They won't do it if the task requires more than a minute or two.

✔ *Do encourage your customers to provide specific details of their transactions.* You'll be hard-pressed to investigate problems (or positives, for that matter) without details relating to who, what, when, and where. Consider designing your comment card so that it asks for these details.

✔ *Do ask customers to provide their contact information.* You may need contact information to clarify details or respond to problems. A telephone number or e-mail address should suffice. Make it clear that the information will not be used for marketing purposes. Don't refuse feedback that fails to include contact information.

✔ *Do put a manager in charge of the comment card system.* If someone with clout oversees the system and monitors it daily, it stands a better chance of achieving its objective: continual improvement and customer satisfaction.

✔ *Do affix postage.* If the comment card is supposed to be returned via postal mail, make sure adequate postage is included.

✔ *Do remind your customers how important their feedback is.* Take the time to remind your customers how much their feedback means to your organization. This message can be especially effective if communicated by the general manager. If customers believe their feedback is important, they'll be more likely to complete a comment card.

✔ *Do communicate corrective actions to your customers.* This is an incredibly powerful practice. It reinforces how seriously you regard customer feedback. It tells customers that they're doing business with an organization that's committed to continual improvement.

✔ *Do whatever it takes to keep a customer.* It's an unfortunate reality that some of the feedback you receive from comment cards will be negative. These can be turned into positives if you remedy the situation immediately. Inducements may be necessary to keep customers that have had particularly bad experiences.

✔ *Do improve the comment card system.* Without a doubt, some of the feedback you receive will relate to the comment card system itself. Take action on what you learn to improve the system and the timeliness and volume of feedback should also improve.

✘ *Don't use the system for collecting marketing information.* If you're going to spend the time to manage a system of comment cards, use it for its intended purpose—gathering customer feedback. Develop a separate system for building your advertising database.

✘ *Don't expect comment cards to provide a representative sample.* By their nature, comment cards will capture the extremes of customer experiences. Don't expect the accumulated data from this tool to reflect organizational performance accurately. The results will be heavily skewed toward the poles—very good and very bad.

✘ *Don't allow employees to coach customers.* The role of most employees regarding comment cards is to let customers know that the system exists, where the cards are located, and how to return the feedback. Coaching customers on the "right" responses is inappropriate.

✘ *Don't put pressure on your customers to complete comment cards.* There's a fine line between educating customers about the system and hounding them. Make the tools available, remind customers that their feedback's important, but leave it at that.

✘ *Don't attach employee rewards to the comment card system.* Over time, a system with rewards attached to it will spur employees to coach customers on which responses to give, and/or badger them to complete the cards. If you decide that employee rewards must be part of the equation, be prepared to provide plenty of education and supervision to your employees.

ANALYSIS AND ACTION

Time is of the essence with a comment card system. The organization must be prepared to analyze and act upon feedback in real time, while the issues are still uppermost in customers' minds. Here are some common-sense steps that will guide the process:

■ Every day, someone with the authority to make decisions and take action must review comment card feedback.

- Problems and complaints must be transferred into the customer complaint system and investigated. If you have the contact information, call or e-mail the customer immediately. Let the customer know that you intend to report back when appropriate corrective action has been taken.
- When feedback reveals positives, recognize employees in a dignified, public manner. Also, make sure that the behaviors or systems that produced the positives are incorporated into formal procedures.
- If possible, input feedback into a database or spreadsheet to facilitate trend analysis.
- Analyze the trends in customer feedback regularly. Slice and dice the data in different ways to see if hidden trends emerge. For example data can be sorted for trend analysis by time of service, day of service, product type, service provider, and geographic area.
- Trends should be rolled into a preventive action for investigation and action.
- Any time that corrective or preventive action has been taken to address a feedback issue, communicate with customers and let them know. Explain the actions that have been taken, and thank the customers for their input.
- Update all formal procedures to include improvements and fixes that have been implemented.

Comment cards, in all their various forms, can be excellent tools for customers to provide "flash feedback" on your organization's performance. These systems require a fair amount of up-front planning, but only simple daily maintenance once they've been launched. Consider pairing comment cards with another feedback system to provide a fully balanced picture of customer perceptions.

Tracking No. _____

THANK YOU FOR YOUR BUSINESS!

We value your business highly, and your feedback is taken very seriously. Please provide specific details of your transaction so that we can make improvements.

Date of Service: ___/___/___	Service Description: _____

Personnel Who Provided Services: _____

Your comments and suggestions (in as much detail as possible): _____

_____

_____

_____

Please provide your name and phone number in case we need to follow up about your feedback. Your contact information will not be used for marketing purposes.

Name: _____	Phone Number: _____

If you have a complaint, please see the manager or contact us immediately at 1-800-XXX-XXXX.

INVESTIGATION AND FOLLOW-UP

Results of Investigation: _____

_____

_____

Action Taken: _____

_____

_____

Corrective and/or Preventive Action No._____ (if applicable)

Was the customer contacted as a result of comment?

❑ Yes ❑ No	(if no, explain: _____)
Date of Contact: ___/___/___	By: _____
Customer Response: _____	

Tracking No. _____

SHIPMENT COMMENT CARD

Your feedback is very valuable to us. Please take a few moments to let us know your satisfaction with this shipment.

Delivery Date: ___/___/___   Product Code (8-Digit): _____

Please mark the box that applies for each statement	Strongly Agree	Agree	Disagree	Strongly Disagree
Product arrived on time.				
Delivery person was courteous.				
Product arrived in good condition.				
Product quality suits my application.				

Please add any additional comments and suggestions you may have (in as much detail as possible):

_____

_____

_____

Please provide your name and phone number, in case we need to follow up about your feedback. Your contact information will not be used for marketing purposes.

Name: _____   Phone Number: _____

Enclose this card in the postage-paid envelope provided and drop in any mailbox.

INVESTIGATION AND FOLLOW-UP

Results of Investigation: _____

_____

_____

Action Taken: _____

_____

_____

Corrective and/or Preventive Action No._____ (if applicable)

Was the customer contacted as a result of comment?

❑ Yes   ❑ No   (if no, explain: _____)

Date of Contact: ___/___/___   By: _____

Customer Response: _____

_____

_____

Chapter 5

Complaint Systems

t's odd to think of a complaint system as a customer satisfaction tool. Complaints indicate the exact opposite of customer satisfaction, right? But that's exactly the point. An effective complaint process should serve as your customer satisfaction warning system. Imagine a big red light mounted on the wall of your conference room. When a customer complains, the light blinks and is accompanied by a deafening buzzer. This is how your complaint system should function.

Obviously, complaints communicate customer perceptions, and perceptions compose the largest determinant of customer satisfaction. The one glaring drawback to complaint systems is their completely reactive nature. You're not reaching out to your customer; the situation is, in fact, reversed. You're relying on the customer to reach out to you. This is a chancy operation. A significant number of customers simply won't take the time to lodge a complaint. They feel their time is too valuable, they don't have confidence in your ability to solve the problem, they've already decided to take their business elsewhere, or any number of other reasons. The bottom line is that you won't ever receive their complaints. For every complaint your organization receives, there are many more you'll never hear about.

Because of its purely reactive nature, a complaint system is something that should be used in combination with one or two other, more proactive, customer satisfaction tools. These will extend the organization's tentacles deep into the environment, while the complaint system will function as the last line of defense. If the proactive systems do their jobs, you'll hear about many issues long before they escalate into a formal complaint. But the complaint system will still be there, like a huge boulder guarding the entrance to your customer satisfaction domain.

POINT OF CONTACT

An effective complaint system must be easily accessible to your customers. A single toll-free phone number is the best mode of contact, even if your organization is large, with multiple facilities. Don't confuse your customers with instructions such as, "If you're calling about our outdoor recreation products, dial the Chuckamucka facility. If you are calling about our watercraft products, dial the Simpleville facility." Give them one phone number, and make sure it's posted prominently in multiple places—the user's manual, assembly guide, packing list, exterior box, invoice, and thank-you note. Make it clear to even the most casual consumer where to call if there's a problem. Don't fret that you're treating your customers like children.

Customers are likely to be irritated when they call about a complaint. Don't put them on hold or send them into voice mail. They will only become more irritated, and this will affect their ability to communicate the details of their problem. Establish whatever kind of staffing or infrastructure necessary so that customers speak to a real person. It's a good investment.

Another communication faux pas is transferring a customer from one telephone extension to another. The employee who answers the call initially should be adequately trained and have the necessary tools for soliciting and recording details of the complaint. If this person isn't able to carry out the task, take whatever actions are necessary to ensure this person can deal with customers' problems. Practicing complaint calls can raise an employee's confidence and improve his or her ability to deal with the customer.

Other communication media, such as fax, e-mails, or Web forms, can function as first points of contact for complaints, but voice contact is still the best. Customers with complaints want to talk to someone, and fast. Speaking directly with a human provides assurance that the problem with be solved and everything will turn out OK.

EMPATHY

Empathy is an important part of dealing with customers who have complaints. What exactly does "empathy" mean? Simply that the person talking to the customer can understand the situation from the customer's point of view. He or she understands why the customer might be upset and is able to share some of the same feelings. An empathetic customer service rep will let the customer know that he or she would probably feel the same way.

Is it appropriate to express regret because of the problem? Sure. The customer has experienced something unpleasant, and it only makes sense to say you're sorry about it. Saying "I regret you had this problem" is not a confession of guilt. You're just saying what one friend or business partner would say to another when something goes wrong. However, the organization's representative should avoid any talk about guilt or fault-finding.

Adding empathy to the complaint process will signal to the customer that he or she isn't alone in the situation. The customer has an ally of sorts. Establishing this is critical to defusing any anger or ill feelings that the customer may possess. Empathy is also the first step toward turning the negative side of the complaint experience into a positive one—and ultimately rebuilding the customer satisfaction that might have been lost.

Empathy simply means acknowledging the emotional aspect of a customer's complaint. Some customers require more than others. Obviously, the more upset and emotional a customer is, the more empathy will need to be applied to the situation. Everyone's communication style is different, but the essential message that most customers want to hear is:
- I can certainly understand how you feel about this situation.
- We regret that you were inconvenienced.
- We will investigate this problem as quickly as possible and let you know what we learn.

Don't go overboard when expressing empathy. The delivery should be calm, dignified, and sincere. Does this come naturally to most people? Rarely. People who are likely to be on the receiving end of complaints should have ample opportunity to practice their responses. It will be time well spent.

GETTING THE DETAILS
Besides expressing empathy, the person receiving the complaint must gather the details. Exactly what went wrong? Allow the customer to provide a general description, then begin to ask for particulars. Typically, these include:
- What was the problem's exact nature? Generalities aren't helpful here. Keep trying to learn the specific details of what went wrong. The problem statement must provide enough detail and depth to facilitate investigation.
- When did the problem occur? The date is certainly necessary, and the time might also be.

- Where did the problem occur? The state, city, plant, retail outlet, department, production line, and machine may all be important.
- Who was involved in the situation? What roles did they play?
- What product was involved? What were the part numbers or style numbers?
- Were there any specific batch numbers, serial numbers, or other identifiers that can be used for tracking?
- Was the problem isolated or generalized across all products?

Gathering this depth of information consistently is difficult without a structured form. Most organizations custom-design complaint forms based on their individual needs. Decide on exactly what information you require to investigate customer complaints and take effective action, then design your form around these needs. Certain sections of the complaint form are almost universal, however. These generally include:

- Person to whom the complaint is assigned
- Response due date
- Root cause
- Actions taken
- Verification of actions taken
- Closure signature and date

It's a very good idea to include proof of follow-up communication as one of the form's requirements. A sample complaint form is shown at the end of this chapter.

PROJECT MANAGEMENT

Each complaint should be assigned to a project manager whose job is to assemble the necessary resources and ensure that all phases of the problem-solving process are carried out. This individual should have the project management skills to ensure that the correct people are involved and that they have the proper tools to address the problem. The project manager should also have the authority to remove barriers and take action. Fill in the "assigned to" space on the complaint form with the project manager's name.

This might sound a little over-managed to some. After all, we're just talking about a customer complaint, right? Yes, but a complaint can be very complicated. Consider all the typical steps that occur when a company responds to a customer complaint:

- The problem is clearly defined.
- The root cause is identified.
- A range of acceptable corrective actions is proposed.
- One of the actions is chosen.
- The action is implemented
- Follow-up occurs to ensure the action was effective.

■ Corrective actions and results are reported to the customer.
■ Procedures and other documentation are updated as necessary to reflect changed methods.

Many more steps could be added, depending on the nature of the complaint. A process as complex as this requires a project manager. Think about all the effective and ineffective corrective actions in which you've been involved. It's likely that with the effective actions, someone (i.e., a project manager) was responsible for driving the project to completion.

Effectively managing customer complaints includes at least three distinctive characteristics:
■ *Clearly assigning ownership.* A project manager should oversee the corrective actions for each complaint.
■ *Defining a problem-solving method.* This is simply a logical, step-by-step process for addressing the problem effectively. The eight steps listed in the preceding paragraph constitute a problem-solving method. A step-by-step problem-solving method facilitates a team approach to investigation and action. Without it, chaos and failure generally result, and the customer gets angrier by the day.
■ *Involving a wide range of personnel.* Managers don't have all the answers. Organizations must capitalize on their personnel's creativity and intelligence when customers complain. Executives, managers, supervisors, operators, trainers, technicians, administrators, and troubleshooters should all be involved in the problem-solving process.

The best complaint systems galvanize the entire organization into action like a fire alarm. In an emergency, such as a fire, everyone has a role in maintaining the organization's collective safety. This is true when a customer complains, too. The more people involved in the complaint investigation, action, and follow-up, the more likely the organization will learn from the experience and not repeat the same mistakes again. Team-based problem solving is a particularly effective tool for involving personnel. This doesn't necessarily mean decision making by committee (usually disastrous); it simply means that a wide range of people are contributing to the solution.

A complaint administrator should be assigned to manage the complaint system. This person has a number of important responsibilities:
■ Supervising the input of information into the complaint database
■ Routing the complaint form to the appropriate project manager
■ Ensuring that fields in the complaint database are updated as investigation and action proceeds
■ Prioritizing the complaint when investigation and action aren't proceeding according to plan

Organizations often assign the job of complaint administrator to someone with little real authority. This is a mistake because it can be misinterpreted as an indication of how inconsequential the customer complaint system really is. The complaint administrator's role is critical and it shouldn't be lightly assigned.

COMPLAINT MANAGEMENT SOFTWARE

Complaint management software can help significantly in tracking and analyzing complaints. The software's complexity and sophistication, however, is worthless if the complaint administrator can't determine the status of all complaints at a glance and easily convert raw data into graphics.

Many complaint management software packages can be bought off-the-shelf, and many of them are effective. It's often cheaper and easier, however, for the organization to develop its own software tools. A complaint database can be developed in a matter of minutes using relational database or spreadsheet software. Complaint databases usually include fields for most of the spaces found on a typical complaint form. It's a good idea to put the complaint database on a server, with read-only access granted to the organization as a whole.

JUSTIFIED VS. UNJUSTIFIED COMPLAINTS

Some organizations classify complaints according to whether they're "justified." This might be considered as logical means of prioritizing complaints, but it's the worst thing an organization could do for building customer satisfaction. As a customer, all my complaints are justified. Why else would I bother complaining? If I'm told that my complaint is "unjustified," that's only going to make me angrier than I already am.

The customer experienced a problem, and now it becomes your problem. Regardless of whose fault the problem is, customer satisfaction has been affected, and we must take action. Consider these scenarios:

■ A customer used the product incorrectly, and its performance was adversely affected; the complaint is unjustified. Response: Why did the customer use the product incorrectly? Was the application known prior to the sale? Were the instructions unclear? Is there any chance that the customer was misled, even unintentionally?

■ A customer says the product was damaged, but the damage described could only have happened at the customer's location; the complaint is unjustified. Response: Should the product's packaging be improved? Should guidelines be provided for proper handling?

■ A customer says the shipment arrived late, but the customer selected the carrier; the complaint is unjustified. Response: Should longer lead times be stipulated when this carrier is used? Should the carrier be contacted on the customer's behalf? Should the customer be assisted in selecting an alternative carrier?

■ A customer says the service person was rude, but this person was provoked by one of the customer's employees; the complaint is unjustified. Response: Should company personnel be trained in dealing with difficult people? Should employees be coached in conflict resolution?

In each of these cases, an argument could be made that the problem was the customer's fault. Taking this position, however, does nothing to enhance customer satisfaction. Nor does it further the organization's long-term objectives. Smart organizations will look for ways to error-proof their products with customers.

Of course, some problems are truly the customer's fault. When these situations occur, the organization might not be obligated to replace the product, provide credits or refunds, or accept returns. In all cases, however, customers must be treated in a diplomatic and cordial manner. They must never be told, "You're complaint is unjustified."

REPORTING BACK TO CUSTOMERS

Humans are naturally curious. If you give someone feedback, it's hard not to wonder what they do with it. This is especially the case with negative feedback based on a purchased product. Customers want to know what action has been taken. After all, the customer had a negative experience. The customer even took the time to tell the product's creators about it. Now the customer is curious. What action has been taken?

If your organization is interested in turning a negative complaint experience into a positive one, someone must take the time to report back to the customer. The communication should include three key elements:
■ The results of the investigation into the problem
■ The actions that have been taken
■ A statement of thanks for reporting the problem

Reporting actions back to the customer brings closure to the issue. It also lets the customer know that you take his or her feedback seriously and are committed to improving. In some cases, this call can make the difference between the customer continuing to do business with you or not.

IMPLEMENTATION PROCEDURES

The following steps represent implementation guidelines for an effective complaint system:
■ *Determine what information is needed to investigate and take action on customer complaints.* Build your complaint form around this information.

■ *Establish contact methods for customer complaints.* Remember that most customers prefer voice contact. Test the contact method in various situations to make sure it works as intended.

■ *Develop a written procedure for handling complaints.* Stipulate responsibilities, authorities, protocols, and problem-solving steps, as appropriate. Refer to the sample procedure at the end of this chapter.

■ *Appoint someone as complaint administrator.* This person will be responsible for entering information into the complaint database and routing complaint forms for investigation and action.

■ *Educate the customer on how to contact the organization in the event of a complaint.* Put the contact information in multiple places.

■ *Train all employees in their roles within the customer complaint system.* Remember that the more people involved in the process, the better your organization's chances for improvement.

DOS AND DON'TS OF AN EFFECTIVE COMPLAINT SYSTEM

Make sure to incorporate into your customer complaint system the following dos, and avoid the don'ts.

✔ *Do make reporting easy.* Specify a simple, user-friendly contact method for customers to use when reporting their complaints. Utilize a toll-free phone number, if possible.

✔ *Do empathize with customers.* Let customers know that you regret the trouble they've experienced. Make them feel like you are on their team, working together to improve the situation.

✔ *Do get the details.* Record all the details related to the complaint on a form of some sort. Without consistently getting the facts on all problems, it will be very difficult to take effective action and rebuild customer satisfaction.

✔ *Do assign ownership.* Assign each complaint to someone who's responsible for managing it to completion. Ownership will ensure that the issue doesn't mysteriously disappear before the problem has been investigated and fixed.

✔ *Do use a problem-solving method.* A structured problem-solving method will ensure a methodical approach to investigation and action on complaints. It will also facilitate the use of a team in problem solving.

✔ *Do get people involved.* Try to utilize a wide range of people in the problem-solving process. The more people participate in problem solving, the more comfortable and effective they will be in the process.

✔ *Do use each complaint as a learning opportunity.* The problem has occurred; your organization might as well embrace the problem as a way to improve. Keep the process positive and make root cause analysis a rallying point for the organization.

✔ *Do error-proff your product.* Make it nearly impossible for customers to make problems for themselves. Brainstorm ways that your customer could misuse or abuse the product; develop controls to prevent these things from happening.

✔ *Do report fixes to your customers.* Your customers are naturally curious about what you've done to address their complaints. Let them know about corrective actions. This highlights how seriously you view their feedback.

✔ *Do ensure effectiveness.* Follow up all actions to ensure they removed the root causes of problems.

✔ *Do build a knowledge library.* Over time, the complaints database can become a knowledge library for the entire organization. The problems of the past can help educate your personnel and prevent problems from cropping up in the future.

✘ *Don't expect full representation.* Your complaint system will not be a true indicator of all existing complaints. A significant number of people aren't going to take the time to complain.

✘ *Don't complicate communication.* Don't frustrate customers by putting them on hold or transferring them from one extension to the next. Customers will only become more agitated.

✘ *Don't jump to conclusions.* Don't attempt to perform root cause analysis on complaints when you're on the phone with a customer. Just get the details and do the investigation later when you can focus on the issues.

✘ *Don't classify complaints as justified or unjustified.* If the customer perceived a problem, then the complaint is justified. There's no such thing as an unjustified complaint (although the organization might not be obligated to give credits or provide replacements in all cases).

✘ *Don't rush complaints.* Don't be afraid of keeping a complaint open for as long as needed in order to take effective action. For some complaints, this might be a day or two. For others, this could be a number of months.

ANALYSIS AND ACTION

When analyzing complaints, the total number of complaints isn't that important. Here's why:

■ The number of complaints recorded by an organization doesn't necessarily represent the true number of complaints, so this quantification is almost meaningless.

■ Once a goal is established for reducing the total number of complaints, it's inevitable that reporting complaints will be discouraged, either consciously or unconsciously. You don't want to do anything to prevent receiving customer feedback, especially negative feedback.

A better way to analyze complaints is to focus on certain types. Analyze complaints according to these criteria:

■ *Pareto analysis of complaints according to a complaint code.* The complaint code is simply a tag assigned to each complaint in the database, so that trends will stand out more clearly. A list of sample complaint codes is given at the end of this chapter. Obviously, each organization must develop its own list of complaint codes geared to the problems faced in its industry.

- *Pareto analysis of complaints by product lines.* This could indicate whether problems appear to be generated by certain products lines or product types.
- *Pareto analysis of complaints by customer.* This could indicate if trouble is localized with a particular customer, which could indicate the need for on-site visits or other special attention.
- *Most expensive complaints.* Analyze complaints according to the dollar amount of their impact. Expensive complaints pose the biggest risk to the organization.

Complaint information should be one of the most widely disseminated topics in your organization. Trend data should be posted on every departmental bulletin board, along with the details of relevant complaints involving that department. Complaints, their root causes, and eventual corrective actions must be the subjects of any regular communication that takes place within the organization.

Top managers should be more knowledgeable about complaints than anyone else. A discussion of complaints should be included on the agenda of any business review meeting. Top managers should review progress toward determining root causes and taking effective actions. When this happens, the complaint system's effectiveness increases significantly, and customer satisfaction stands a chance of improving.

CUSTOMER COMPLAINT REPORT

Customer: _____   Date Reported: ___/___/___   Complaint No.: _____

Customer Location: _____   Contact Person: _____

Phone Number: _____   E-mail: _____

Complaint Description: _____

Complaint Code: _____   Product Serial Number(s): _____

Sales Order No.: _____   Bill of Lading No.: _____

Quantity to be Returned: _____   RA No. (if applicable): _____

Complaint Project Manager: _____   Response Due Date: _____

Investigation and Action (Attach additional sheets if necessary)

Root Cause: _____

Corrective Action: _____

Team Members: _____

Completed By: _____   Date: ___/___/___   Estimated Date of Completion: ___/___/___

Follow-Up for Effectiveness

Reviewed By: _____   Date(s): ___/___/___

Actions Effective?:   ❏ Yes   ❏ No   Results of Actions: _____

Reporting to Customer on Investigation and Action

Customer Contacted By: _____   Date: ___/___/___   Person Contacted: _____

Customer Response: _____

Closure

Complaint Closed By: _____   Date: ___/___/___

COMPLAINT CODE—REV. 3

Code	Description
WRG	Wrong product shipped
DST	Shipped to wrong destination
LTE	Late shipment
DMG	Product arrived damaged
RDE	Rude or discourteous driver
LBL	Labeling problems
OPR	Operating problems
PHY	Product failed physical tests
HOL	Final product had holes
INV	Invoice incorrect

(Note: Complaint codes facilitate classification of complaints according to theme. These are presented as examples only. Each organization must develop its own complaint codes based on its own and industry circumstances.)

CUSTOMER COMPLAINT PROCEDURE

1. Purpose/Scope

The purpose of this procedure is to provide a consistent manner of recording, investigating, and taking effective action on customer complaints for all types of goods and services. Its ultimate objective is to restore customer satisfaction that may have been affected by the complaint.

The guidelines set forth in this document cover all company locations. Any questions should be directed to the quality manager.

2. Definitions

2.1. Customer complaint: A perceived problem with a good or service reported by an external customer.

2.2. Complaint administrator: The individual who is responsible for ensuring the overall functioning of the complaint system. The quality manager serves as the complaint administrator.

2.3. Project manager: The individual who is assigned responsibility for managing the investigation and action on a particular customer complaint.

3. Initiation of Complaints

3.1. External customer complaints normally will be received by customer service personnel via the published toll-free phone number.

3.2. Information about the complaint will be recorded on a customer complaint report (Attachment 1) by customer service. The top portion of the report should be completed, as applicable. The customer complaint report is then forwarded to the complaint administrator.

3.3. The complaint administrator will assign a complaint number to each complaint and enter the complaint details into the complaint database.

3.4. The complaint administrator assigns a complaint project manager to each complaint. The complaint project manager is contacted via phone or e-mail to discuss the assignment.

3.5. Copies of the customer complaint must be forwarded to the appropriate sales representative and business group manager.

4. Investigation and Action

4.1. The complaint project manager will assemble the necessary personnel and resources to investigate the complaint.

4.2. Team-based problem solving will be employed whenever possible, using the prescribed eight-step

CONTINUED

problem-solving method. The names of the team members will be recorded on the complaint report, if applicable.

4.3. The root cause will be identified and recorded on the complaint report. Actions taken to address the root cause will also be recorded.

4.4. The complaint project manager is responsible for reporting the status of the complaint to the complaint administrator by the "response date" shown on the complaint report.

4.5. Investigation and action on the complaint will continue until the project is declared completed by the complaint project manager. The customer complaint report will then be returned to the complaint administrator.

4.6. The complaint administrator, or his or her designee, will update the complaint database for all actions

5. Verification of Effectiveness

5.1. The complaint administrator, or his or her designee, will follow up to verify effectiveness and determine the results of actions.

5.2. The results of the follow-up will be recorded on the complaint report. The complaint database will also be updated to reflect effectiveness and results of actions.

6. Reporting Results to Customer

6.1. The complaint administrator, or his or her designee, will contact the customer representative to report on the results of the complaint investigation and action. The customer should be contacted within 60 days of the complaint's initiation, even if investigation of and action on the complaint is not yet completed.

6.2. The customer's response will be recorded on the customer complaint report. Additional observations by the person contacting the customer may also be recorded.

6.3. Expressed dissatisfaction with the action taken will be brought to the attention of the applicable salesperson and business group manager.

7. Closure

7.1. Upon satisfactory evaluation of the action on the complaint and the customer's response, the complaint administrator will close the complaint. The complaint database will be edited to indicate closure.

7.2. Copies of the closed complaint must be forwarded to the appropriate sales representative, business group manager, vice president of sales, and the president.

8. Analysis

8.1. The complaint database maintained by the complaint administrator will be used to identify trends, compile summaries, and provide input into business review meetings and other meetings, as appropriate.

Chapter 6

Quantitative Customer Surveys

Quantitative customer surveys are by far the most complex customer satisfaction tools described in this book. The quantitative customer survey is usually the first tool that springs to mind when people think of methods for gauging customer satisfaction. As a result, many organizations will attempt a quantitative customer survey as their initial foray into the realm of measuring perceptions. However, jumping right into this method is almost always a mistake.

First, let's back up and precisely describe the quantitative customer survey. It generally embodies the following attributes:

- A series of questions or statements about the product
- A response scale that follows each of the questions or statements
- Reduced emphasis on open-ended questions that solicit qualitative responses (though including a few open-ended questions is recommended)
- A survey tool (also referred to as a questionnaire) that presents the questions and records the responses

Here's an example of the type of question that might appear on a quantitative customer survey:

How would you describe the professionalism of our sales representatives?

1	2	3	4	5
Very Poor	Poor	Adequate	Good	Very Good

An alternative format presents the customer with a statement, then asks the customer to respond with the degree to which he or she agrees with the statement:

Our sales representatives act in a professional manner.

1	2	3	4	5
Strongly Disagree	Disagree	Neutral	Agree	Strongly Agree

When designed and administered correctly, quantitative customer surveys offer a number of advantages:

- Surveys can be sent anywhere. Geographical distance isn't a limitation.
- Respondents can remain anonymous. This often results in more candid responses. (Anonymity doesn't apply to telephone or in-person surveys, of course.)
- All issues are presented in exactly the same way to all customers.
- Responses can readily be tabulated and statistically analyzed.
- Results paint a comprehensive and balanced picture of the organization in the eyes of its customers, instead of revealing only the extremes of opinion.
- Results can be converted easily to graphics, which facilitates their interpretation.
- Results can be compared to previous surveys to reveal broader performance trends.

This tool seems remarkably straightforward, and the benefits certainly recommend its use. So why are quantitative surveys a mistake to implement as a first attempt in the customer perceptions process? Because a quantitative customer survey is expensive, time-consuming, and difficult to administer. It's easier to begin with a less complex method, then move to quantitative surveys after you've exploited the simpler tools to their fullest extent. These will also sharpen your understanding of key satisfaction variables, and this knowledge will help you construct a more effective quantitative survey.

For those who are ready to implement a quantitative customer survey system, this chapter looks at some of the important considerations to keep in mind.

PRELIMINARY INFORMATION

A number of identifiers will aid in categorizing and analyzing responses later in the survey process. These are generally the questions that launch the survey, and they'll differ from industry to industry and company to company. The challenge is to determine which identifiers will be most helpful in understanding the responses and targeting your organization's improvement efforts. Examples of these identifiers include:

■ Male vs. female respondents
■ Number of years as a customer
■ Type of product typically purchased
■ Typical place of purchase
■ Typical method of contacting organization

These questions will be accompanied by scales that require customers to check one of the responses, as opposed to asking them to write in an answer. Here's an example of this type of question as it might appear on a survey:

How many years have you been our customer?
☐ < 1 year
☐ 1–2 years
☐ 3–5 years
☐ 5–10 years
☐ >10 years

There's a limit to how many questions of this type you can ask, so it's critical to nail down exactly which identifiers will provide the richest opportunities for later analysis.

ASKING ABOUT THE RIGHT SATISFACTION ISSUES

The range of customer satisfaction variables is virtually limitless. You can ask your customers about courtesy, professionalism, timeliness, responsiveness, availability, reliability, conformity, performance, or other issues. But typically your customers care about a smaller set of product attributes. Sure, your customers would like everything about the business experience to be perfect, but it's their relatively short list of core issues that determines whether they'll remain customers. Do you know what these issues are? Most organizations don't. So, instead of trying to find out what matters most to their customers and building their surveys around those issues, they ask their customers about everything.

Some quantitative surveys ask more than one hundred questions. Customers simply aren't going to take the time to answer a survey spanning multiple pages. Think about your own experiences: How many customer surveys have you received, only to ignore or toss them out? Your customers will do the same unless you narrow the issues and shorten the survey's length.

Field reports, call reports, comment cards, and other tools can assist in narrowing the field to the most important issues. This is primarily why it makes sense to start with these tools first. For example, you may learn through your call reports that your products' packaging and labeling are more important to your customers than you expected. You can then highlight packaging and labeling issues on the quantitative survey.

If you had a choice, you'd certainly prefer to ask customers about every possible variable related to customer satisfaction. But you can't. Customers simply don't have the time or the patience to complete a long, comprehensive survey. Narrowing the issues will ensure a higher response rate and provide you with more relevant information. No more than about ten issues should be represented on a survey tool—although more than ten questions might address these issues. These should easily encompass the important topics from the customer's perspective. A list of issues and corresponding statements and questions are included at the end of this chapter.

The other important consideration related to the range of issues concerns their "actionability." In other words, are you willing to take action on everything you ask about on the survey? Don't ask about your product's price competitiveness if that's something that you're not willing to change.

In summary, the themes addressed by your survey will fall into two main categories:

■ Issues your customers care about the most
■ Issues you're willing to act upon

Obviously, issues will change over time, so a quantitative customer survey will evolve just like the other tools described in this book.

CREATING EFFECTIVE SURVEY QUESTIONS

Once the key survey issues have been identified, the individual questions and/or statements must be formulated. This is much harder than it seems. Some people even suggest that writing survey questions is an art form, and that's not far from the truth. The difficulty stems from the fact that what you intend when you write the questions might not be what the reader interprets when he or she reads them. Your message gets lost, and you're not there to explain what you meant. So each question must stand on its own, without the need for clarification.

The problem of respondent misinterpretation is one the biggest obstacles to quantitative customer surveys. Because responses are usually scaled, customers don't get a chance to improvise open-ended answers. They must guess at what you meant, and the survey results will reflect their confusion. Statistical tools are available for validating survey questions, but following the simple guidelines listed here will achieve the same end. For simplicity's sake, the term "question" is used for both questions and statements:

■ *Clearly indicate exactly what or who is being evaluated.* Provide enough identifiers so that there's no ambiguity.
- *Bad question:* How would you describe our communication? (What communication are you asking about?)
- *Better question:* How would you describe the communication skills of our customer service representatives? (This statement is clearer.)

■ *Don't ask more than one question at a time.* Divide questions and/or statements so that only one attribute is being evaluated in each one.
- *Bad question:* How would you describe the product knowledge and courtesy of our customer service representatives? (You're asking about two attributes at the same time, which will only confuse the response.)
- *Better question:* How would you describe the product knowledge of our customer service representatives?

■ *Use words that all respondents will understand.* A quantitative survey is no place to impress people with your vocabulary. Keep the language and sentence construction simple.
- *Bad question:* Quotes are returned in an expeditious manner. (Respondents might not know what "expeditious" means. This might cause them to throw the survey away or give an answer inconsistent with the word's true meaning.)
- *Better question:* Quotes are returned quickly.

■ *Ask about specific attributes, not generalities.* Don't ask questions that summarize a number of product attributes into a single, sweeping declaration.
- *Bad question:* Our customer service representatives really know how to serve their customers. (What's being asked about here? The question is too vague.)
- *Better question:* Our customer service representatives work hard to answer all product questions.

Once you've written questions that meet these basic conditions, ask a handful of trusted colleagues or customers to review the survey and provide feedback. Carefully consider all criticisms. Continue refining the questions and statements until you're certain they address the issues in the clearest, most direct manner possible. (A list of sample statements and questions is included at the end of this chapter.)

SCALING THE QUESTIONS
Each survey question is followed by a scale that allows respondents to record their perceptions. The scale you decide to use will depend on the type of questions you've created.

Survey questions (e.g., "How would you describe the reliability of our circuit boards?") are followed by a scale indicating subjective qualities: poor, fair, good. Survey statements (e.g., "The reliability of our circuit boards is among the best in the industry") are followed by an agree/disagree scale. Beyond these general guidelines, scale choice becomes more complicated. The factors to be considered are:

- Balance between resolution and simplicity
- Logical flow
- Clearly defined scale points

The scale must provide enough resolution (i.e., measurement gradations) to reveal true differences in the measurement. A scale with two points (e.g., agree and disagree) provides very little resolution, whereas a scale with twelve points provides a great deal. The trick is to strike a balance between resolution and simplicity.

With a quantitative customer survey, the measuring instrument isn't the scale; it's the person responding to the questions. The scale merely provides a structured way for the person using the survey to record his or her feedback. When selecting a survey scale, you must ask yourself, "Do my customers have the powers of discrimination necessary for the scale I'm proposing?" The reality is that most humans can respond quite accurately to a two-point scale (e.g., go/no-go, agree/disagree, yes/no), but uncertainty increases quickly as additional points are added to the scale.

A five-point scale strikes a reasonable balance between resolution and simplicity. More than five points introduces complexity that doesn't pay off in additional information. Humans simply don't possess the accuracy or precision of a pair of calipers, so a response scale with a multitude of choices is unnecessary.

An effective scale must also have a logical flow. In other words, the points' meaning should represent progressive gradations from the worst to the best (or vice versa) or from completely disagreeing to completely agreeing (or vice versa). The following scale does not provide a logical flow because the points jump around:

1	2	3	4	5
Strongly Disagree	Strongly Agree	Disagree	Agree	Neutral

An effective scale must also possess equal distances between each point. As one point progresses to the next, the reader should perceive equivalent intervals. The scale below doesn't possess equal distances between points because of the large cognitive gap between the second and third responses. In other words, the gap between "Needs Improvement" and "Excellent" is larger than the gaps between any other pair of points:

1	2	3	4
Poor	Needs Improvement	Excellent	Outstanding

Another consideration is the scale's bias. Do the choices represent a full range of opinions, from one extreme to the other? The following scale is biased toward positive responses. If someone wants to provide a response more negative than "Fair," they're out of luck—no such response exists:

1	2	3	4
Fair	Good	Excellent	Outstanding

The final issue related to flow is the direction in which the scale moves. Pick a direction and stick to it. Most scales flow from left to right, with the left-most point representing the most negative or most disagreeable response, and the right-most point representing the most positive or most agreeable response. The opposite will work fine, too. Just don't switch back and forth. If they appeared on the same survey tool, the two following scales could prove confusing to the user. On the first scale, the left-most point represents the most favorable response, but on the second, the left-most point represents the least favorable response:

1	2	3	4
Excellent	Good	Fair	Poor

1	2	3	4	5
Strongly Disagree	Disagree	Neutral	Agree	Strongly Agree

Scales should always have defined points. These should either be defined at each point or coded in such a way that the definitions can be located in a nearby key. Points should never be left undefined, relying on the responder's interpretation skills. Undefined points only introduce additional elements of uncertainty into the survey process, which effectively increases measurement error. Here's an example of a scale that doesn't define all the response points:

1	2	3	4	5
Strongly Disagree				Strongly Agree

When points are left undefined, you're assuming that your customers can read your mind regarding the meaning of each point. This is a very poor bet. Make sure to define all response points.

The scales used in this book are referred to as Likert scales, named after Rensis Likert, who developed the concept during the 1930s. A list of scales and a discussion of each are included at the end of this chapter.

DESIGNING THE SURVEY TOOL

Let's face it: appearances matter. This fact also applies to customer surveys. A cluttered, complicated-looking survey will be tossed into the trash faster than you can say "standard deviation." Time spent designing the survey will be an excellent investment. No matter how well the survey questions are written, if someone is intimidated by the how it looks, you'll have wasted your time. Here are some general thoughts on designing an effective survey:

■ *Collect customer surveys every chance you get.* Ask your friends and colleagues if their companies have used a survey. Benchmark good ideas from the surveys you collect. Also make a list of the things you don't like. Designing a survey is much easier if you have some examples. (Two examples are included at the end this chapter.)

■ *Keep the length to two pages or less.* Strive for one page. If it's a voice survey, make sure it can be administered in ten minutes or less.

■ *Make the font size large enough to read easily.* Anything smaller than a ten-point font will pose problems for some people. If the questionnaire will be faxed, pay special attention to the font size and letter spacing. Printed materials' resolution and clarity degrade rapidly when faxed.

■ *Don't use unusual fonts* (e.g., script or novelty). Strive for something that's easy to read.

■ *Keep a space at the top for the questionnaire's number.* This space will stay blank until the completed questionnaire is returned to your organization. Numbering each of the questionnaires as they arrive will facilitate data tabulation and verification.

■ *Include brief instructions at the top of the survey.* These will vary, depending on the survey's content but here's an example: *Please respond to each statement by circling the rating that most accurately describes your perception. Provide only one response for each question. If you accidentally mark more than one, please draw an X through the incorrect response.*

■ *Include a few basic identifiers.* These are for identifying the type of customer that completed the survey and will provide additional angles for later analysis.

■ *For more expansive surveys, especially those using agree/disagree scales, include up to three statements about each satisfaction issue.* Each statement should approach the issue from a different angle. Including multiple statements about the same issue helps to verify your customers' interpretations of the issues and might give you more accurate responses.

■ *Don't place questions and/or statements addressing the same issue next to each other.*

Spread the questions around so you receive unbiased responses. You don't want the customer to think: "Oh, I see. They're asking me about the same type of thing again." Your use of multiple questions about the same issue shouldn't be obvious to the customer.

■ *Questions and/or statements with the same scale should be grouped together.* Don't flip back and forth between scales unless you want to confuse the customer and receive erroneous responses.

■ *Somewhere within the survey, include a list of all the issues the survey addresses.* Ask each customer to rate the issues in terms of importance. A fine example of this is shown in the Diamond Manufacturing Co.'s survey at the end of this chapter. Here's another example as it might appear toward the end of a survey. This example focuses only on the top three most important issues: *From the list below, please mark the three issues you consider to be the most important. Put a 1 beside the most important issue, a 2 beside the second most important issue, and a 3 beside the third most important issue. Please don't mark more than three issues:*
☐ Friendliness of staff
☐ Responsiveness to problems
☐ Availability of service

■ *Include one or two open-ended question related to satisfaction.* For example, "What would you like to see us do better in the future?" or "Please give us advice on how we can better meet your needs." Provide plenty of space for feedback.

■ *Include this final question in every survey:* "What would you recommend that we do to improve this survey?" Again, provide plenty of space for feedback.

■ *Number each of the questions and/or statements.* This will facilitate data tabulation once the completed questionnaires are returned.

■ *Consider using a graphic designer's services.* It's important that your survey look as professional and organized as possible.

As with so many other aspects of conducting a survey, it's important to seek opinions from people you trust. Design a draft survey and ask colleagues to provide feedback. Don't let the first survey go out the door until you're confident it will do the job you want. Otherwise, you're wasting your customer's time, and that does nothing to increase satisfaction.

SAMPLING

Sampling refers to exactly how many people will receive and (hopefully) complete the survey. To a lesser degree, it also refers to exactly who will complete the survey at the organization to which it's sent. Let's first examine the greater issue of how many people will receive surveys.

Sampling helps you understand the characteristics of an entire population (in this case, your customers) while only surveying a portion of that population. Sampling, as opposed to a 100-percent inspection, lowers the cost of administering and tabulating data. If the sample is selected using statistically valid principles, reasonably accurate inferences about the broader population can be drawn from the sample responses. The main variables in selecting sample sizes for a customer survey include:

- *Confidence level.* How confident would you like to be that the sample results represent the larger population? As your confidence requirements increase, so must the sample size. A reasonable confidence level for surveys is ninety-five percent.
- *Confidence interval.* How wide a tolerance will you accept around the individual results within the survey? As the tolerances tighten, the sample size goes up. We will use plus-or-minus four percent confidence limits in this chapter.
- *Randomness of sample.* Samples selected must be random for them to represent the larger population effectively.

A detailed discussion of statistics is beyond this book's scope, but a range of sample sizes is provided below. They're based on a ninety-five-percent confidence level, plus-or-minus four percent confidence interval, 0.5 proportion, and random selection. The sample sizes correspond with the total number of customers.

Total customers	Sample size	Total customers	Sample size
20	20	750	334
50	47	1,000	376
100	86	2,000	462
150	121	3,000	501
200	151	4,000	522
300	201	5,000	537
400	241	10,000	567
500	273	50,000	595
600	301	100,000	597

Thanks to Michael Stamp for his assistance in the development of this table.

Responses based on these samples provide a ninety-five-percent confidence level and plus-or-minus four percent confidence intervals, as stated previously. This means that if sixty-seven percent of customers rate your customer service employees' courtesy as "excellent," you could say that you're ninety-five-percent certain that between sixty-three percent and seventy-one percent of all customers (based on the plus-or-minus four percent confidence interval) believe the courtesy of your customer service employees is excellent.

Once the sample size has been determined, the organization must select the specific customers who will receive surveys. Selecting customers must be made on a purely random basis. The organization must fight the tendency to over-sample the big, important, or high-margin customers. A random number table and/or generator—available in many statistics books and on Web sites—can assist in ensuring a random sample, particularly in cases where companies have established a "customer number" for each of their clients. Even if the organization hasn't established customer numbers, sales order numbers or case numbers can be used in tandem with the random number generator. Don't leave randomness up to someone's good intentions.

You must now decide who within the customer's organization will be surveyed. This is the specific individual who will communicate his or her perceptions via the survey tool. Selecting these people should not be done randomly, unless you want a low response rate. Carefully decide who you believe is best prepared to provide accurate feedback. This might be the customer's executive manager, purchasing agent, department manager, production supervisor, operator, or warehouse supervisor. The issues represented in the survey often dictate who within the customer organization needs to receive the survey.

One final note on sampling: The sample size shown in the table above is the completed sample. You'll have to send out significantly more surveys than the number shown. A twenty-percent response rate is considered very good in most surveys. Given that rate, you'd have to send out 1,500 surveys to receive 300 completed surveys. So make sure you consider the nonresponse factor when planning the number of surveys that will actually be sent.

To summarize, keep these steps in mind when planning your sampling strategy:
1. Determine the sample size based on the total number of customers
2. Randomly select customers to be surveyed
3. Carefully select who within the customer's organization will be asked to complete the survey
4. Realize that not everyone will respond, so send out at least five times more surveys than you need to fulfill the desired sample size.

NOTIFYING CUSTOMERS

Nobody likes surprises within the course of their business day. They generally mean extra work. Don't surprise your customers with a survey. Regardless of the survey type (e.g., mail, telephone, fax, or e-mail), it will be better received if the customer knows it's coming.

A simple letter, e-mail, or phone call will suffice in giving your customers due warning. Make sure to address the communication directly to the person who ultimately will receive the survey. The communication should include a number of distinct components, including:

- *A description of what to expect.* Let the person know whether the survey will be administered via postal mail, e-mail, telephone, fax, or some other means.
- *When the survey will arrive.* Specifying a window of time is generally adequate.
- *The survey's purpose.* Of course, the purpose is to make improvements and become a better supplier.
- *The importance of feedback.* Make sure to emphasize how much their honest feedback means to your organization.
- *Desired completion date for the survey.* Don't make demands. Simply ask them to complete the survey by the date specified.
- *Whom they can call if they have questions, comments, or if they don't want to take part in the survey.* Always give the customer the option of not participating.
- *Whether they can expect to receive summarized results of the survey sometime in the future.* (Don't even mention this if you're not sending out results.)
- *The signature of the highest-ranking manager at the organization administering the survey.* It's also a good idea to have the letter co-signed by the customer's contact person (e.g., sales or customer service).

Providing this communication in advance may seem like extra work, but it will increase your response rate and shorten the delay in getting feedback. A sample notification letter is included at the end of this chapter.

GIVEAWAYS AND GOODIES

Some companies have had success in offering their customers giveaways and goodies to entice them to complete a survey. Some of these enticements include discounts on future purchases, free samples, and token gifts. Keep in mind, however, that giveaways can significantly increase the survey's cost. If your organization elects to try this, strike a balance between enticements that have value to the customer and those that won't place an overwhelming burden on the organization. Educating the customer about the survey's purpose often gives equal results as providing enticements.

BEGINNING THE SURVEY

Now you're finally ready to administer the survey. When all the other preparations have been done correctly, this step is fairly anticlimactic.

Attach a very brief cover letter to each survey, thanking the customer for participating. The letter should also remind the customer how to return the completed survey and when the desired due date is. Make sure to reference the earlier communication regarding the survey. Follow the survey with a self-addressed, stamped envelope for its return. The whole thing should fit into an oversized envelope which is stamped with "Customer Survey Enclosed" and/or "Thanks in advance for your feedback." As with the notification letter, the envelope is addressed directly to the person who will be expected to complete the survey.

Here are some other general guidelines to ensure the process goes smoothly:
- *Telephone surveys.* Call the customer within the time period promised on the notification letter. Before beginning the questionnaire, ask the customer if it's a convenient time to do so. Be prepared to juggle your schedule to accommodate the customer. Remember, the customer is doing you a favor by providing feedback. The least you can do is be flexible.
- *E-mail surveys.* Keep the e-mail simple. Don't include flashy graphics that will take a long time to load. If you're attaching files, make sure that everyone you're sending the survey to has the correct software for opening the file; this can be one of the issues addressed in the notification letter. Include straightforward instructions for saving the files and returning them. If the e-mail includes a link to a Web site where the survey is located, test the link to make sure it works.
- *Fax surveys.* Make sure that the fax is readable upon transmission. Send a few test faxes to verify this.
- *All surveys.* Try to send out all the surveys within the same time frame, usually a two- or three-day window. This ensures that all respondents have about the same amount of time to complete the survey and respond.

THE REMINDER LETTER

Within two weeks of distributing the survey, send a reminder letter to everyone who received the survey. This can take the form of a postcard, letter, e-mail, or fax. The letter's purpose is twofold:
- Thank the customer for participating in the survey
- Remind them of the desired due date and ask them to complete the survey if they haven't already.

You're trying politely to motivate all those who put the survey on the corners of their desks, then promptly forgot about it. Some organizations believe so strongly in reminders that they send out two: the first within two weeks of the survey being sent, and a second around the four-week mark. With two reminders, you run the risk of irritating your customers, particularly those who responded promptly. A sample reminder letter (postcard style) is included at the end of this chapter.

<h2 style="text-align:center">COLLECTING DATA</h2>

Responses will start coming in soon after the survey has been distributed. You must decide exactly what will happen to the data when it arrives. During the planning process, appoint someone to be the data administrator. This person will enter the survey data into a computer. A clerical task, yes, but a very important one. It's so important that the data administrator role is often assumed by the person in charge of the entire survey process. Regardless of who performs the duties, the data administrator must be detail-oriented, disciplined, and comfortable working with the computer. When they arrive back at the organization, completed surveys should immediately be forwarded to this person.

Data can be directly input into spreadsheet software such as Lotus 1-2-3 or Excel. There are more sophisticated statistical software tools that aid in collecting and analyzing data, but spreadsheet software will work just fine for the kind of analysis I recommend. Spreadsheet data can easily be exported into other software packages if that's desired later.

The spreadsheet can be set up and populated in this way:
- Column A is labeled "Survey No." This tracks the sequential number of each completed survey, as assigned by the data administrator, when it arrives back in the organization. The data administrator writes the number on the survey, then enters it into the spreadsheet.
- Column B is labeled "Date." This is the date that each completed survey arrived back in the organization. Multiple surveys may have the same arrival date, but each will have a different survey number.
- Column C lists the "identifiers" from the survey. In the example shown, this column contains responses from the question, "How many years have you been a customer of ours?" The responses are coded so that less than one year equals 1, one to two years equal 2, three to five years equal 3, five to ten years equal 4, and more than ten years equal 5. For simplicity's sake, this is the only identifier shown in the example, but your organization may capture additional identifiers as part of the survey.
- Column D and those that follow it will track the numbered questions and/or statements from the survey. Each column following will be numbered according to the questions and/or statements. As completed surveys arrive, the data administrator enters the ratings assigned by the customer for each question and/or statement.

The table below illustrates what a spreadsheet of this sort might look like. There's nothing difficult about populating it. The most critical element is accurately entering data. If mistakes are suspected later in the process, the data in the spreadsheet can always be verified with the data on the individual surveys via the survey number that appears in both places. However, careful keying will eliminate the need for later verification.

	A	B	C	D	E	F	G	H	I	J
1	Customer Survey—March 2003									
2				Question Number						
3	Survey No.	Date	Years	1	2	3	4	5	6	7
4	1	03/15/02	1	3	4	2	3	3	4	2
5	2	03/16/02	1	3	3	2	3	3	3	1
6	3	03/16/02	2	4	4	3	4	2	3	2
7	4	03/16/02	4	3	3	2	3	2	2	3
8	5	03/17/02	2	4	3	3	4	3	3	2
9	6	03/17/02	3	4	3	3	3	3	3	2
10	7	03/17/02	3	4	4	3	3	4	4	3
11	8	03/17/02	1	4	3	3	2	3	3	1
12	9	03/18/02	2	3	3	2	3	2	2	2
13	10	03/18/02	1	2	3	2	2	3	2	2

ANALYSIS

Data analysis can easily mire the survey process if you let it. You may slog through the statistical swamps for so long that you forget the survey's purpose. The purpose, of course, is to take action and increase customer satisfaction. This fact sometimes gets lost in the intricacy of crunching numbers.

Keep the analysis simple. Focus especially on graphic representations of data. These are understood by almost anyone—including top managers—and the easier the interpretation the more likely it is the organization will make improvements. Researchers at the Centers for Disease Control need sophisticated statistical techniques; you probably just need to figure out where your biggest improvement opportunities are.

A wide variety of methods exist for evaluating survey results, but I'm going to present one that's very simple and effective.

Calculate the average response for each survey question. This can be accomplished by typing the formula for average. For example, using Microsoft Excel, the formula would be: *[first row-last row]/total number of surveys returned*. The formula can be copied across to all columns.

Rank each question in terms of average response, from smallest average to largest. If the scales all possessed the same logic (e.g., 1 represents the least favorable response and 5 represents the most favorable), then the ranking would be meaningful. Here's an example of what this ranking would look like graphically, showing the ten least-favorable responses. Questions eighteen and four seem to pop out as prominent opportunities for improvement.

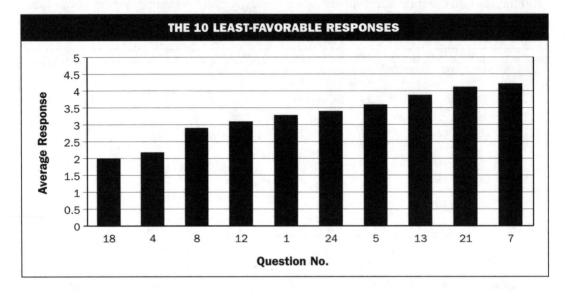

Next, calculate the three most important issues, as reported by the customer. This can be accomplished by establishing a new worksheet. Put each issue in a column, with the survey numbers listed in each row. You'll need to convert the customer's response in this way: If the customer marked an issue as a 1 for most important, enter a 3 in the worksheet under the corresponding issue. If the customer marked a 2 for second most important, enter a 2 in the column for that issue. If the customer marked a 3 for third most important, enter a 1 in the column for that issue. Do this for every survey that's returned. Add the total importance rankings under each issue, and you'll have an idea of what customers believe are the most important issues. A simplified version of this analysis is shown at the top of the following page.

	A	B	C	D	E	F	G
1	**Most Important Issues, as Reported by Customers**						
2	3 = most important, 2 = second most important, 1 = third most important						
3	Survey No.	Availability	Responsive-	Courtesy	Problem-	Service	Speed of
4			ness		Solving	Effectiveness	Service
5	1	1				2	3
6	2			1	2		3
7	3	1				2	3
8	4		1		2		3
9	5			1		2	3
10	6			2	1	3	
11	7		1	2			3
12	8	1				2	3
13	9			1	2	3	
14	10	1				2	3
15	SUMS	4	2	7	7	17	24

Obviously, you'd have more than ten completed surveys to include, and these satisfaction issues probably won't represent the themes that your organization will decide to highlight on a survey, but you get the idea.

The analysis of issue importance indicates that "service effectiveness," with a total score of seventeen, and "speed of service," with a total score of twenty-four, are the two most critical issues in customers' minds.

You must now cross-reference the issues with the survey questions representing each issue. In our hypothetical example, it turns out that question eight, with the third-lowest score, addresses service effectiveness, and questions twelve and twenty-four—those with the fourth- and sixth-lowest scores, respectively—address speed of service.

So, despite the fact that questions eighteen and four seemed to pose the biggest opportunities, the issues they address simply aren't that important to customers. You wouldn't have known this without including the ranking of issue importance on the survey tool. With this information in hand, you can:
- Form teams to address the issues of service effectiveness and speed of service. Make sure team leaders are selected.
- Brainstorm actions to improve performance related to these issues.
- Implement the most promising actions and manage progress through to completion.

Of course, there are more sophisticated ways of analyzing customer surveys. If your organization possesses the means and expertise to carry out this kind of analysis, then by all means use them. However, most organizations don't possess such resources. The best use of their time and effort, then, is to pinpoint opportunities and take action.

Another way of identifying opportunities is to look at responses with respect to the identifiers that appeared on the survey. For example, if you asked, "How many years have you been our customer?" as an identifier, you could analyze satisfaction responses by years as a customer. Analysis of this sort is exploratory. You might (or might not) have a hunch that a relationship exists between customer longevity and satisfaction. The point is to slice the data in a number of directions, and see what kind of hidden relationships may exist.

IMPLEMENTATION PROCEDURES

The following steps summarize the key activities to follow for an effective quantitative customer survey:

1. Learn which satisfaction issues are the most important to your customers. Simple tools such as call reports, field reports, and comment cards can facilitate your understanding of what customers really care about.
2. Draft questions and/or statements that reflect customers' most important issues.
3. Assign appropriate scaling to each question and/or statement.
4. Determine the identifiers that will provide additional depth during analysis. Examples include product line most often purchased, number of years as a customer, and male vs. female respondent.
5. Design the survey. Make sure it's readable, uncluttered, and appropriate for the method of delivery to the customer.
6. Select an appropriate sample size based on the total number of customers, your desired confidence level, and desired confidence intervals.
7. Make sure that the customers chosen to fulfill the sample size are selected randomly.
8. Notify customers that they'll receive a survey. Request a specific date for its completion and return. Allow customers the opportunity to opt out.
9. Begin the survey process. If surveys are sent directly to customers (as is the case with mail, e-mail, and fax surveys), make sure they all go out within the same time frame.
10. Send out reminder letters, as appropriate.
11. Appoint someone to the position of data administrator. This individual must be detail-oriented, disciplined, and comfortable working with a computer.
12. Enter survey responses into a spreadsheet as they're returned to the organization.
13. Analyze the data using the method described in the analysis section above. Use additional methods if statistical competency exists within your organization.
14. Take action on the most promising opportunities or ominous threats.
15. Track progress of actions until they're complete.

DOS AND DON'TS OF QUANTITATIVE CUSTOMER SURVEYS

Keep the following points in mind as you implement and manage your quantitative customer survey:

✔ *Do get feedback on questions.* Solicit feedback on survey questions and statements before putting them on the survey. No questions should be included on the survey until you are certain that they are clear and concise.

✔ *Do sanity-check the scales.* Make sure that the scales are balanced and logical, with equal intervals between each point. Also make sure that each point on the scale is defined. Avoid highly subjective words that could have multiple meanings (such as "OK").

✔ *Do design an attractive survey.* The more attractive and user-friendly the survey is, the more likely people are to respond.

✔ *Do allow customers to rate importance.* Include a section on the survey for each customer to rate issues in terms of importance. This will help in prioritizing the improvement opportunities that are identified.

✔ *Do include instructions.* Customer surveys should always have instructions. Make them clear and simple. Consider providing a phone number for customers to call if they have questions about the survey.

✔ *Do get help.* Consider using outside resources for the design, implementation, and analysis of a quantitative customer survey. It's a complicated process that can be aided greatly by external expertise.

✔ *Do send out plenty of surveys.* Remember to consider the nonresponse rate when sampling customers. Send out up to five times more surveys than you need to fulfill your desired sample size.

✘ *Don't ask about the impossible.* Don't ask about issues that you are unwilling or unable to act upon. This only establishes unreasonable expectations in the minds of customers. Unreasonable expectations always damage customer satisfaction.

✘ *Don't ask about everything.* Avoid the temptation to cover every possible variable of satisfaction on your survey. Focus on the critical drivers of satisfaction, which are typically no more than ten issues.

✘ *Don't overanalyze.* Don't become overly entranced by statistical analysis of survey results. Do the necessary analysis, but focus on action and improvement.

✘ *Don't start with a quantitative survey.* Don't implement a quantitative survey until you have fully utilized the simple tools for gathering customer feedback.

SAMPLE QUESTIONS AND/OR STATEMENTS

The following survey questions and statements are arranged by theme. The survey statements would be matched to an agree/disagree scale. The survey questions would be matched to a judgment scale (e.g., poor, fair, average, good, excellent). The purpose of providing these statements and questions is to spur your own thought process. With a little time and creativity, you'll be able to develop items much better than these.

Overall performance

I will purchase from this organization in the future.
I would recommend this company to a friend.
I'm very satisfied with the service I receive from this company.
This organization is a model of how to serve customers.
This company is dedicated to customer satisfaction.
I plan to be a long-term customer of this organization.
Doing business with this company is always a smart decision.
The products are world-class.
This company is the best in the industry.
I'm proud to do business with this organization.
How is our performance overall?

Accessibility

I'm able to contact the organization when I need to.
I never worry about reaching a service person.
It's easy to get in touch with the organization.
I don't get put into voice mail.
The company makes it easy to contact a service representative.
Personnel are always on call when I need them.
How would you describe our accessibility?

Attractiveness

Products supplied by this company always look good.
The products are visually appealing.
I like this company's products because they're striking.
Beautiful is a word I would use to describe these products.
I like to look at these products.
How would you rate the attractiveness of our products?

Availability of goods and services

The lead times quoted to me are always adequate.
Products are rarely out of stock.

CONTINUED

Service is available in the desired time frame.
A service person is always available when needed.
I can get products when I need them.

Billing

Invoices arrive when they're supposed to.
Invoices are always accurate.
I don't get frustrated by this company's billing process.
I understand all the details that appear on my invoice.
I don't think that the company tries to deceive me through confusing billing.

Cleanliness

Cleanliness is something that the employees seem to care about very much.
The facility is exceptionally clean.
Employees obviously take pride in cleanliness.
I never see litter or refuse on the grounds.
The facility is among the cleanest I have seen.
How would you describe the cleanliness of our facilities?

Communication

Communication with employees is very clear.
I always understand what is being said.
Confusion never results from conversations with employees.
It's easy to initiate communication with the organization.
Talking with employees is pleasant.
Communication problems are quickly resolved.
How well do we succeed in communicating with you?

Conformity

The product consistently meets the specifications.
Tolerances are never exceeded.
The product is exactly what I ordered.
The product meets my requirements.
The service was performed in the way I wanted it.

Convenience

It is convenient to do business with this organization.
Buying from this company is easy.

CONTINUED

Convenience is one of the key reasons I am a customer of this company.
This company has locations where I need them.
Employees try to keep me from being inconvenienced.
This organization operates with my convenience in mind.

Courtesy

Employees are very courteous to me.
The customer service representatives always seem happy to talk to me.
Rudeness is never an issue.
I am always greeted as an important customer.
I am consistently treated with the respect.
Employees never "talk down" to me.
This organization makes me feel like a friend.

Delivery performance

The product arrives when it's supposed to.
Late orders are a rare occurrence.
I am always notified if a delay is expected.
The company consistently provides a product when it is promised.
Delivery personnel are courteous.

Design

The product works well for its intended application.
This company designs excellent products.
Products have the features I want.
I am impressed by the design of this company's products.
Products are designed with the proper functionality.
This company seems to read my mind when it designs a new product.

Discretion

My business is kept private by employees.
Nobody within the organization has ever betrayed my confidence.
I don't hesitate to share information with employees because I know they will guard it.
The organization can be trusted with my valuable information.
My privacy is never in question when I do business with this organization.

Durability

Products supplied by this company are tough.

CONTINUED

Indestructible is a good description for these products.
I'm not afraid of wearing out these products.
I can confidently tackle any job with the products supplied by this company.
Things I buy from this organization are very durable.

Effectiveness

The products do what they're supposed to do.
Service is consistently effective.
This product works better than competing products.
The product gets the job done.
Personnel are effective in assisting me.

Empathy

I never feel that the company doesn't care about me.
Employees of this company are "on my side."
I feel that personnel can relate to my difficulties.
This organization knows what I have to go through.
Employees of this company really care about me.

Ethics

This organization is very ethical.
I believe this company obeys all laws that apply to it.
Ethics are a key value of this organization.
Employees uphold high ethical standards.
I have no reason to believe that this company does anything unethical.

Fun

I have fun when I come here.
This place makes me smile.
Employees act like they want me to have a good time.
Fun is a word I would use to describe my interactions with this company.
I always leave here happy.
It's not unusual for me to laugh when I'm a customer here.

Helpfulness

Employees are always interested in helping me.
I never have to search for someone to help me.

CONTINUED

This company is dedicated to helping me be more successful.
I always feel that I receive the proper help when I am a customer.
How would you describe the helpfulness of our employees?

Innovation

This organization is always developing new and exciting products.
Products are on the cutting edge.
Competing products are less innovative.
I'm a trendsetter when I use these products.
The employees of this company think in innovative ways.
This company is a trailblazer.
How would you describe our ability to develop new products you need?

Knowledge

Employees always know what they're doing.
Personnel have a firm grasp of their jobs.
I am never faced with ignorant employees.
This company seems to make sure its employees are well-trained.
Employees have the necessary knowledge to assist me.
How would you describe the knowledge of our employees?

Labeling

The product always arrives with the desired labeling.
Product labeling is clear and readable.
There is never any question about the identity of products when they arrive.
Labels do not fall off.
The labeling is durable.

Maintainability

The products are easy to maintain.
Maintenance is not difficult.
Spare parts are easy to obtain.
These products require less maintenance than competing products.
These products require very little upkeep.

Packaging

Packaging is well-suited to the product.
The product never arrives damaged.

CONTINUED

Packaging materials are easy to recycle or dispose of.
The product's packaging facilitates its handling and shipping.
Packaging is not excessive.

Prestige

I would rather be seen using one of this company's products.
The use of this company's products means I have achieved high status.
People recognize that this organization represents excellence.
No other products afford me the prestige I get from these products.
I feel better about myself when I use these products.

Pricing

Pricing of products is fair.
I consider product pricing to be competitive.
The price of services match the benefit I receive.
I'm satisfied with the price I pay for these products.

Problem solving

Personnel are able to quickly identify the root causes of problems that arise.
The organization is dedicated to effective problem solving.
Problem prevention is a core value of this company.
When something goes wrong, employees are quick to fix it.
Personnel have creative solutions for addressing problems.
I have confidence in the problem-solving abilities of this organization.

Professionalism

The employees of this company conduct themselves professionally.
Everybody I deal with has a polished manner.
I feel like more of a professional when I deal with this organization.
This company is more professional than its competitors.
Professionalism is one of the core values of this organization.
Employees have never said or done anything I consider to be unprofessional.

Quotes

Quotes are provided quickly.
Quotes include all the information I need.
The amount quoted rarely changes later during the project.
I feel that the organization does a good job of quoting its services.
When I receive a quote, I'm confident that I know the exact cost.

Reliability

I don't have to worry about these products breaking down.
Product failures are rare.
Repair is never an issue because these products are so reliable.
The reliability of these products is one of their biggest strengths.
How would you describe the reliability of our company's products?

Responsiveness

The company is very responsive to my needs.
When a problem comes up, personnel act quickly to address it.
I'm always called back promptly.
I feel that the organization responds well.
Personnel quickly swing into action to address my needs.

Safety

I feel safe when I use these products.
Using this product does not pose unusual hazards for me.
Instructions adequately address safety features.
Getting hurt is not something I worry about when I use this product.
I have never been injured using this product.
I don't feel unsafe when I come to your place of business.
I feel comfortable bringing my family here.
All necessary safety features are standard with the products.

Sex appeal

I feel sexy when I use this product.
The use of this product makes members of the opposite sex desire me more.
This product increases my sex appeal.
The company knows how to incorporate sex appeal into its products.

Style

Products provided by this organization have a distinctive flair.
I feel stylish when I use these products.
People know I'm very cool when they see me using these products.
This company sets the style in the industry.

Technical support

Technicians know their products inside and out.   **CONTINUED**

This organization makes sure its personnel have the proper technical expertise.

I'm impressed by the technical competence of employees at this company.

Outstanding technical support is one of the reasons I am a customer.

Technical support is always effective.

How would you describe our technical support?

Value

The products I purchase from this company represent good value to me.

I get my money's worth when I do business with this organization.

Buying from this company is a wise business decision.

The cost of the services is overshadowed by their value.

SURVEY SCALES

The following scale is the most commonly used for survey statements (e.g., "Please indicate your level of agreement or disagreement with the following statement: Quotes are always received in a timely fashion.") The scale covers the full range of responses, has a logical flow, and is balanced.

❏ 1 Strongly Disagree	❏ 2 Disagree	❏ 3 Neutral	❏ 4 Agree	❏ 5 Strongly Agree

The following scale is used when respondents are asked how satisfied they are with a particular satisfaction variable (e.g., "Please indicate your level of satisfaction with the following aspects of our performance...")

❏ 1 Very Dissatisfied	❏ 2 Dissatisfied	❏ 3 Neither Satisfied nor Dissatisfied	❏ 4 Satisfied	❏ 5 Very Satisfied

The following scale would be appropriate for survey questions asking for a subjective judgment (e.g., "What is your opinion of our performance in the following categories?"). The scale's middle point is neutral, and there are equal intervals between points.

❏ 1 Poor	❏ 2 Fair	❏ 3 Neutral	❏ 4 Good	❏ 5 Excellent

This is a variation of the previous scale. It recognizes that sometimes "poor" is not the worst performance possible. Some people bristle at the inclusion of a powerfully subjective word like "horrible," but "excellent" is also a very strong and subjective word.

❏ 1 Horrible	❏ 2 Poor	❏ 3 Adequate	❏ 4 Good	❏ 5 Excellent

This is a variation on the scale used when respondents are asked for their subjective judgments. One of its strengths is its simplicity and its ability to discourage the tendency of some respondents to choose the middle point.

❏ 1 Poor	❏ 2 Fair	❏ 3 Good	❏ 4 Excellent

This is a very simple, three-point scale based on customer expectations. Its main strength is its ability to quickly focus on problems.

❏ 1 Did Not Meet Expectations	❏ 2 Met Expectations	❏ 3 Exceeded Expectations

The following scale would be used when a question asks how the organization compares to its competitors. It has a balanced flow and includes the full range of responses.

❏ 1 Far Worse	❏ 2 Worse	❏ 3 About the Same	❏ 4 Better	❏ 5 Much Better

The following scale would be paired with questions that ask to what degree the product met requirements (e.g., "To what degree did the widgets meet your assembly requirements?"). The scale points correlate closely to Poor, Fair, Good, and Excellent.

❏ 1 Not at All	❏ 2 Somewhat	❏ 3 Mostly	❏ 4 Completely

The following scale is probably the clearest and least ambiguous one for recording a subjective judgment. All points are balanced by an equal and opposing point on the contrasting end, and the middle point is completely neutral.

❏ 1 Very Poor	❏ 2 Poor	❏ 3 Neither Good nor Poor	❏ 4 Good	❏ 5 Very Good

SAMPLE CUSTOMER SURVEYS

Two sample surveys are shown on the following pages. The surveys represent widely divergent products—industrial goods and medical services—but they both represent lean and effective approaches for implementing a customer survey.

Diamond Manufacturing Co.—Wyoming, Pennsylvania

www.diamondman.com

This company performs precision perforating on metal, plastics, and other materials for a variety of customers in a diverse range of industries. Diamond's survey encompasses eleven performance areas, and uses a five-point scale for customer responses and ratings of issue importance. The survey includes two open-ended questions and finishes with a few questions related to electronic commerce and special communications media.

Dr. Brett Saks—Chandler, Arizona

http://www.holistic-physician.com

Dr. Saks, a doctor of chiropractics, uses this customer survey to gauge his effectiveness in treating patients and meeting their expectations. The survey is short and punchy, using a five-point agree/disagree scale (plus an extra point for statements that aren't applicable). Three open-ended questions are included at the bottom. The issues cover the full range of patient satisfaction variables, but the length is kept to a single page.

CUSTOMER SATISFACTION SURVEY

|We appreciate your business and want to continue to satisfy your needs. To ensure that we understand what they are,
|how well we have met them in the past, and what we need to do to keep your business in the future, we ask that you
|complete this survey. A token of our appreciation will be sent to you upon receipt of your reply. Thank you.

Please rate each item in terms of 1) how important it is to you and 2) our performance:

	Importance To You					Our Performance				
	Great	High	Medium	Low	None	Excellent	Good	Average	Fair	Poor
Adequacy of Information (Catalog/Website)	5	4	3	2	1	5	4	3	2	1
Helpfulness of Customer Service	5	4	3	2	1	5	4	3	2	1
Technical/Engineering Assistance	5	4	3	2	1	5	4	3	2	1
Quote Response Time	5	4	3	2	1	5	4	3	2	1
Pricing of Product	5	4	3	2	1	5	4	3	2	1
On-Time Delivery of Product	5	4	3	2	1	5	4	3	2	1
Packaging	5	4	3	2	1	5	4	3	2	1
Quality of Product	5	4	3	2	1	5	4	3	2	1
Response to Questions/Concerns/Problems	5	4	3	2	1	5	4	3	2	1
Effective Calls/Visits by Sales Rep	5	4	3	2	1	5	4	3	2	1
Overall Ranking as a Supplier	5	4	3	2	1	5	4	3	2	1

Please expand upon any of the questions above and/or complete the following statements (optional):

Diamond is our perforator of choice because...

Diamond would be a better supplier if...

Please answer the following questions relating to e-commerce:

I can access the internet from my work computer?   Yes   No

If yes, I would submit orders/check order status on-line if it were secure & easy to use?   Yes   No

I prefer to submit request for quotes/orders via (circle all that apply):   mail   phone   fax   e-mail   on-line

I prefer to receive quotes/confirmations via (circle all that apply):   mail   phone   fax   e-mail   on-line

Our company has video confrencing cababilities?   Yes   No   Not Sure

Completed by:_____   Title:_____   Company:_____

p/ 800.233.9601   f/ 570.693.3500   perf@diamondman.com   www.diamondman.com   ISO-9002

243 West Eighth Street, PO Box 174, Wyoming, PA 18644 USA   600 Royal Road, Michigan City, IN 46360 USA

Brett Saks, DC, FAACP, FIAMA

Dynamic Chiropractic & Acupuncture Clinics, PC

PATIENT SATISFACTION QUESTIONNAIRE

Please read each statement carefully. On the line next to each statement, please circle the number which best describes your opinion about the statement.

Strongly Agree	Agree	Neutral	Disagree	Strongly Disagree	N/A
1	2	3	4	5	6

1 2 3 4 5 6   1. I'm very satisfied with the care that I receive.
1 2 3 4 5 6   2. My doctor sees me within 15 minutes of my scheduled appointment time.
1 2 3 4 5 6   3. My doctor listens to me.
1 2 3 4 5 6   4. The doctor's office is conveniently located.
1 2 3 4 5 6   5. The services I receive meet my expectations.
1 2 3 4 5 6   6. My doctor treats me with respect.
1 2 3 4 5 6   7. My doctor suggests exercises and lifestyle changes for me.
1 2 3 4 5 6   8. My doctor does a good job of explaining my condition to me.
1 2 3 4 5 6   9. My doctor is thorough.
1 2 3 4 5 6   10. My doctor's office hours fit my schedule.
1 2 3 4 5 6   11. I am only billed for co-payments by my doctor.
1 2 3 4 5 6   12. The care I receive from this doctor is very good.
1 2 3 4 5 6   13. My doctor is compassionate.
1 2 3 4 5 6   14. Parking is convenient.
1 2 3 4 5 6   15. My doctor's staff is very nice to me.
1 2 3 4 5 6   16. My doctor asks me about other treatment that I have received.
1 2 3 4 5 6   17. My doctor's office is clean and orderly.
1 2 3 4 5 6   18. The doctor explains the reason for the tests and procedures.

COMPLIMENT:_____

_____

COMPLAINT:_____

_____

IMPROVEMENTS FOR FUTURE: _____

_____

OPTIONAL: Patient's name _____ Phone # _____

**Please use other side of this form if you need more space to write.

**Please use the postage-paid envelope to mail to this address:

4939 West Ray Road, Ste. 7 Chandler, AZ 85226

© 2002 Dr. Brett Saks, DC

SAMPLE NOTIFICATION LETTER

January 15, 2003

ACME Products Inc.
100 Marietta St.
Atlanta, GA 30332

Blowhard Corp.
Mr. Aero Gant
117 Central Industrial Row
Atlanta, GA 30332

RE: Customer Survey

Dear Mr. Gant:

I just wanted to let you know that ACME recently designed a customer survey, the purpose of which is to improve our overall operations and become a better supplier. We would very much like you to participate in the survey process.

Around the week of February 5, you will receive the two-page survey via postal mail. Please take a few minutes to complete the survey. It should consume no more than about ten minutes of your time. A self-addressed, stamped envelope will be included for your response, and all responses will be anonymous. If you have any questions about the survey or if you would not like to participate, please call me at (800) 768-2983.

Thank you in advance for your help. Your input to this process is extremely valuable to us. We intend to analyze the results of the survey and initiate a number of improvement projects, with the ultimate aim of increasing your satisfaction with our products and services. You will receive an executive summary of the survey results within six months. Again, thanks for your help.

Best Regards,

Craig Cochran

SAMPLE REMINDER POSTCARD

Dear Survey Partner,

As you know, we began a process of surveying our valued customers about two weeks ago. If you've already completed and returned the questionnaire, let me extend my sincere thanks. It is much appreciated.

If you haven't completed and returned the questionnaire, I urge you to do so. Your feedback is a key part of our plan for making improvements, and with it we intend to become a better supplier. The ultimate result of you providing feedback to us will be your own heightened success.

Thanks again for your help.

Yours in business success,

Craig Cochran
ACME Products Inc.
(800) 768-2983

Chapter 7

In Conclusion

The system for collecting and acting upon customer perceptions is one of the most important systems an organization can implement. What could possibly be more important than learning what your customers think, and taking action to improve your performance in their eyes? Approach the task with the correct amount of discipline, creativity, and resourcefulness, and you will be successful.

It's worth reviewing some of the key points made earlier in the book, so that you can incorporate them in the development of your system:

- ■ *Top management must lead*. Top management must acknowledge the critical and strategic nature of customer satisfaction, and communicate this to everyone in the organization. If top management doesn't believe in the process and truly use it for decision making, nobody else will either.
- ■ *Start simple*. Rely on the simpler tools for gathering customer perceptions first, then move onto more sophisticated techniques.
- ■ *Train personnel*. Train all employees who will be involved in the effort. Let them know how they fit in and what their responsibilities are. Don't leave anything to chance.
- ■ *Utilize existing customer interactions*. You are already interacting with your customers in many different ways. Find ways to turn these interactions into methods for gathering perceptions.

- *Don't over-survey your customers.* Begin capturing customer perceptions, but don't harass your customers. It's easy, especially during the early, enthusiastic days of a newly implemented system, to ask questions about perceptions so often that your customers become annoyed. Go slowly and capture feedback incrementally.

- *Focus on open-ended feedback at the beginning.* As tempting as it might be to develop a quantitative survey right out of the blocks, open-ended tools will provide the best information at the onset of the system. The information gained from open-ended questions will help develop and sharpen your understanding of the important issues in the minds of your customers.

- *Convert perception data into graphics.* Analyze data on customer perceptions, but don't overdo it. The best kind of analysis for this is usually a simple graphic representation of the data. It's much easier to interpret data in graphical form.

- *Take action on what you learn!* Taking action is the most important step in the system; unfortunately, it's also one of the final steps in the system. Don't run out of gas before you've taken action. Failure to act is failure, period. Use basic project management techniques (e.g., assigning responsibilities, clear deliverables, and regular updates) to ensure that actions are followed through to completion.

- *Report actions back to customers.* Customers want to know what you do with what they tell you. It's human nature to be curious, particularly when someone is spending money on your products.

- *Continually improve your system for gathering and acting on customer perceptions.* Over time, you'll learn what works well and what doesn't. Your system should be in a constant state of change and improvement. Making revisions doesn't mean you didn't get it right from the start, it just means you're managing your system correctly.

Does it sound simple? It should. Now go and find out what your customers really think about your products and services. You're competitors will be unhappy that you did.

Bibliography

Deming, W Edwards. *Out of the Crisis*. Cambridge, MA: Massachusets Institute of Technology, Center for Advanced Engineering Study. 1986.

Feigenbaum, Armand G. *Total Quality Control* (Third Edition). New York: McGraw-Hill, Inc. 1983.

Hayes, Bob E. *Measuring Customer Satisfaction*. Milwaukee, WI: ASQ Quality Press. 1992.

Juran, J. M., and Gryna, Frank M. *Quality Planning and Analysis*. New York: McGraw-Hill Inc. 1980.

Index